THE INVESTED LIFE

JOEL C. ROSENBERG
& DR. T. E. KOSHY

THE

INVESTED

making disciples of all nations
one person at a time

Tyndale House Publishers, Inc.
Carol Stream, Illinois

LIFE

Visit Tyndale online at www.tyndale.com.

Visit Joel C. Rosenberg's website at www.joelrosenberg.com.

Learn more about T. E. Koshy's ministry at www.friendshipevangelism.org.

TYNDALE and Tyndale's quill logo are registered trademarks of Tyndale House Publishers, Inc.

The Invested Life: Making Disciples of All Nations One Person at a Time

Copyright © 2012 by Joel C. Rosenberg. All rights reserved.

Designed by Dean H. Renninger

Published in association with Trident Media Group, LLC, 41 Madison Avenue, Floor 36, New York, NY 10010.

Library of Congress Cataloging-in-Publication Data

Rosenberg, Joel C., date.
    The invested life : making disciples of all nations one person at a time /
Joel C. Rosenberg and T.E. Koshy.
        p. cm.
    ISBN 978-1-4143-7637-0 (sc)
    1. Discipling (Christianity) 2. Witness bearing (Christianity) 3. Spiritual formation.
I. Koshy, T. E. (Thottukadavil Eapen), 1933-   II. Title.
    BV4520.R648 2012
    248'.5—dc23   2012016942

Printed in the United States of America

18   17   16   15   14   13   12
8   7   6   5   4   3   2

God offers you eternal life.
He wants you to live an abundant life.
He calls you to the invested life.

THE GREAT COMMISSION

Jesus came up and spoke to [His disciples], saying, "All authority has been given to Me in heaven and on earth. Go therefore and make disciples of all the nations, baptizing them in the name of the Father and the Son and the Holy Spirit, teaching them to observe all that I commanded you; and lo, I am with you always, even to the end of the age."

JESUS CHRIST (MATTHEW 28:18-20)

Table of Contents

How to Use This Book

Get a big, biblical vision.
This is God's heart for his children and his church.

Fear not.
With God's help, you can do this.

Start praying.
Unless the Lord builds the house, the workers labor in vain.

Take baby steps.
Begin with small, manageable tasks: each chapter title is a task; when you finish reading the whole book, go back to the table of contents to see the simple process you can follow.

Note to the Reader

For simplicity, this book generically uses the terms *he* and *him*. But this should not be taken to imply that the invested life is only for men. God's plan for making disciples is universal, with older men investing in younger men and older women investing in the lives of younger women.

Discussion Questions

For your convenience, the discussion questions at the end of each chapter are available online in a printable format. Go to **www.tyndale.com/the-invested-life** and click on the Discussion Guide link along the left.

CHAPTER ONE
ASK TWO SIMPLE QUESTIONS

Go therefore and make disciples . . .
JESUS CHRIST (MATTHEW 28:19)

Every follower of Jesus Christ should be able to answer two simple questions:

- First, "Who is investing in me?"
- And second, "Whom am I investing in?"

God desires to pour an abundance of spiritual and emotional capital into your life—directly and through older and wiser believers. And he wants to use you to pour spiritual and emotional capital into the lives of others. Along the way, you'll be changed. Others will change. You'll grow. Others will grow. You'll feel loved. Others will feel loved. You will experience God and his community in a new and personal and supernatural way. And so will others.

1

God calls this process of spiritual investing "making disciples." It's the heart of the Great Commission. It's the vision of a great local church. It's the secret of a healthy, joyful, secure, and significant life.

We call it "the invested life." And that's what this book is all about.

God the Investor

God is in the business of turning nothing into something and a little into a lot.

In Genesis 1 and 2, we read the story of God creating the heavens and the earth out of nothing. And man out of dust. And woman out of man. And God said it was "good."

In John 2:1-11, we read the story of a wedding where Jesus turned six stone jars of water—each holding between twenty and thirty gallons—into fabulous wine.

In Luke 9:10-17, we read the story of Jesus turning five loaves of bread and two fish into enough food to feed at least five thousand people.

That's the greatness of our great God. He can turn nothing into something and a little into a lot.

And that's exactly what he wants to do in your life.

Think about it. Once you were nothing. Then suddenly, in the blink of an eye, you were born into this wonderful and mysterious world we call the human family. Once you were spiritually lost and alone. Then suddenly you found eternal life. You were miraculously born again and transformed into a member of God's own family.

The apostle Paul puts it this way: "Remember that at

that time you were separate from Christ . . . without hope and without God in the world. But now in Christ Jesus you who once were far away have been brought near through the blood of Christ. . . . Consequently, you are no longer foreigners and strangers, but fellow citizens with God's people and also members of his household" (Ephesians 2:12-13, 19, NIV).

But wait. It gets better. Not only does God want to turn your nothingness into something, he also wants to turn what little human capital you think you have into more than you could ever hope for, dream of, or imagine. He not only wants to give you eternal life; he also wants to give you an *abundant* life.

Jesus said so himself in John 10:10: "I came that they may have life, and have it abundantly"—that it might be significant and meaningful.

The question is, what does an abundant life look like?

"You did not choose me, but I chose you," Jesus explains in John 15:16 (NIV). Why? Why did Jesus choose us? What is it that he wants for us? To make lots of money? To have lots of toys? To have fame or power or worldly success? No. Jesus said, "I chose you [to] go and bear fruit—fruit that will last."

Aha! The abundant life, according to Jesus, is a fruitful life.

What, then, is a fruitful life? The Bible gives us two answers to that question. First, there's the fruit of your changed character, what Paul describes in Galatians 5 as the "fruit of the Spirit"—love, joy, peace, patience, kindness, goodness, faithfulness, gentleness, and self-control. As you abide in Christ Jesus and love him so dearly that you're willing to do what he asks of you no matter what the cost, you will begin to bear the fruit of Christlike character. You will then begin to experience the deep sense of joy and personal satisfaction that comes from pleasing the very heart of God.

Second, Jesus wants you to bear the fruit of winning souls to God's Kingdom and helping them grow to spiritual maturity. Consider Paul's passion for bearing "fruit" by preaching the gospel in Rome (Romans 1:13), as he had with the Colossians (Colossians 1:6), and how he described new converts to Christ as the "first fruits" in 1 Corinthians 16:15. Consider, too, the parable of the seed and the sower in Matthew 13 and Mark 4. Jesus told the story of a farmer who went out to sow seeds in his field. Some fell along the path. Some landed on rocky places. Some fell among the thorns. But some of the seeds fell on good soil, where they produced a crop that was much greater than what was planted. The seed represents the gospel message, and "the seed falling on good soil refers to someone who hears the word and understands it. This is the one who produces a crop, yielding a hundred, sixty or thirty times what was sown" (Matthew 13:23, NIV).

A fruitful person is one who hears the gospel and the Great Commission—a call to a life of knowing Christ, making him known, and helping people grow in their faith—and follows wholeheartedly. In the process, not only is he saved and transformed, but he also helps many others discover God's love and plan for their lives. This is the invested life. Jesus invests in us. We invest in others. And in the process, God turns nothing into something and a little into a lot.

The invested life requires taking risks. There's no way around it. Only one thing's for sure: you can't win if you don't play.

In Matthew 25:14-30, Jesus told the parable of the talents. He explained that the Kingdom of God is like a wealthy CEO who, as he is departing on a journey, entrusts his capital to the wise stewardship of his associates. To one, he entrusts five "talents," worth more than $5,000. To another, he entrusts two talents, more than $2,000. To a third, he entrusts one talent, or more than $1,000.

A long time later, the wealthy man returns from his journey. He wants to know what kind of return he has received on his money. The first associate explains that his investments doubled in value. His five talents have turned into ten talents. Wow. A 100 percent return. Not bad. The second associate also explains that his investments doubled in value. True, he began with less capital, just two talents. But now he has four. He also secured a 100 percent return. Impressive. To each of these associates, the wealthy CEO says, "Well done, good and faithful servant! You have been faithful with a few things; I will put you in charge of many things. Come and share your master's happiness!" (Matthew 25:21, 23, NIV).

The third associate, however, has a completely different story. He tells the CEO that he was afraid to make investments of any kind, even conservative investments. Instead, he hid the CEO's money in the ground. The wealthy CEO fires that man immediately, saying, "You wicked, lazy servant! So you knew that I harvest where I have not sown and gather where I have not scattered seed? Well then, you should have put my money on deposit with the bankers, so that when I returned I would have received it back with interest" (Matthew 25:26-27, NIV).

Is God's primary focus here to encourage us to pay more attention to our financial portfolio? Not in this parable. Instead, God is encouraging us to pay more attention to our spiritual portfolio. His main point is not that we should focus on multiplying his money (though we should definitely be wise and faithful stewards of his resources); his point is that he wants us to focus on knowing him more deeply, obeying him more faithfully, multiplying the number of men and women in his Kingdom, and developing the spiritual depth and character of his children.

In this story—and in a similar one Jesus tells in Luke 19:12-27—we learn that God invests in us, and he expects us to invest in others. If we obey—if we agree to live the invested life—then we will please the heart of God and experience spiritual abundance and joy in this life and in the life to come. But if we refuse—if we hide or spend what he's given us rather than properly investing it—we will find ourselves feeling empty and alone and experiencing God's displeasure.

Spiritual investing requires risk. But with risk comes extraordinary reward.

———

Which brings us to our subject: making disciples.

Christianity is not a solo sport. It's about building strong, healthy teams of fully devoted followers of Jesus Christ whom God can use to change the world. It's about older believers taking younger believers under their wings to love them, help them grow in Christ, and help them reproduce their faith in the lives of *other* younger believers.

That's what Jesus did. He prayerfully recruited a team of young men. He invested in them. He cared for them like family, loving them with an everlasting, sacrificial love. He led them on spiritual adventures. He modeled a life of intense prayer. He let them see supernatural answers to their prayers. He gave them assignments—to feed the hungry, care for the sick, comfort the brokenhearted, and preach the good news of the Kingdom of Heaven. He treated them like sons, correcting their mistakes, praising their successes, and marking their progress. And then he told them to go invest in others. He told *his* disciples to go make *more* disciples. He told them to build warm and loving and nurturing and spiritually reproducing communities called the local church. And in the process he ignited the greatest spiritual revolution the world has ever seen.

This is the essence of Matthew 28:19-20, commonly known as the Great Commission. Jesus said, "Go therefore and make disciples of all the nations, baptizing them in the name of the Father and the Son and the Holy Spirit, teaching them to observe all that I commanded you; and lo, I am with you always, even to the end of the age."

The problem is that nearly two thousand years later, remarkably few Christians are able to point to a single disciple they have made or are in the process of making. Indeed, many would be hard-pressed even to define what is meant by the phrase "make disciples."

Jesus did not come to make "Christians." The world gave us that nickname (Acts 11:26). Jesus came to make *disciples*.

Therefore, it isn't enough to win men and women to Christ, although obviously that is an essential first step. We must also build people up in Christ. We must also *invest* in them until they are fully devoted followers of Jesus, able to help others come to Christ and become fully devoted followers as well. This requires training Christian leaders—vocational ministers as well as lay leaders and volunteers—to see themselves as investors. After all, key to Christ's definition of *success* in ministry is that we produce *successors*, disciple makers who produce still more disciple makers.

How is it possible, then—for all the emphasis in the church these days on winning souls to Christ and world missions—that so many Christians have missed the centrality of personal, intentional discipleship in God's plan and purpose for his people? How is it that we have more and more *seeker* churches but so few *investor* churches, churches committed to helping Christians achieve a healthy balance of evangelism *and* discipleship in their daily walk with the Lord?

It's not just "baby" Christians—young and inexperienced in the ways of God—who are not being discipled or who are not beginning to learn the importance of discipling others. Far too often it is "mature" believers—those who have known Christ for quite some time and whose lives may be busier than ever with ministry activity—who don't seem to understand the importance of discipleship. Indeed, in our experience, we find that many pastors and church leaders have never been personally discipled and have yet to discover how exciting and transforming and fulfilling it is to be discipling their staffs and teaching them how to disciple laypeople, particularly young people.

Which brings us back to you. How would you answer these two simple questions?

1. Who is investing in you?
2. Whom are you investing in?

Is there someone you can specifically point to who has personally and individually taken you under his wing to teach you the basics of the faith—the assurance of salvation, how to study the Bible for yourself, how to develop a prayer life, the importance of fellowship, how to share your faith, and the centrality of pouring your life and faith into someone younger in the faith than you?

Is there currently someone in your life who is meeting with you regularly—in a group and one-on-one—encouraging you to go deeper in your relationship with God? Is there someone who is helping you discover and develop your spiritual gifts, keeping you accountable, listening to your cares and concerns, teaching you how to let God reign in every area of your life, showing you how to maintain a balance of priorities and to make more time to retreat with God, and praying for your needs and for you to bear fruit that will last?

In short, is someone *investing* in you for the long haul?

If your answer is no, then this book can help you. In our experience, so many believers—regardless of their age or spiritual maturity—secretly yearn for someone to reach out to them, care for them, and lead them someplace supernatural, into the very presence and power of our almighty God. We suspect you do too.

If your answer is yes—you have been discipled—that's

wonderful. Relatively speaking in this generation, you're one of the blessed few.

Now the question is, whom are you discipling?

Are you systematically and intentionally building personal relationships with younger believers, helping them master the basics of the faith, helping them establish a firm biblical foundation, and building a faith and ministry on that foundation that will survive the tests of time and difficulty?

Having tasted the sweetness of fellowship with Jesus Christ, are you helping others discover who he really is, what he really wants to do in and through their lives, and how to help still others make these amazing discoveries?

If you are currently engaged in the exciting work of making disciples, then our fondest hope is that this book will serve as a useful tool in your life and ministry and that you'll feel comfortable to share these stories, Scriptures, and principles with others.

If you have never discipled someone—or aren't currently doing so—then our prayer is that this book will motivate you to help fulfill the Great Commission, to experience the joy that comes from developing deep, personal friendships that will last a lifetime, and to do the will of the Lord, who said, "If you love Me, you will keep My commandments" (John 14:15).

Seven Ways This Book Can Help You

The Bible is the ultimate blueprint for making disciples and building the local church because it alone is the ultimate authority on the life and ministry of Jesus Christ, our supreme model.

This book does not purport to be the only approach to discipleship. It is, instead, intended to be an encouragement to those studying God's Word to discover the practical secrets of being a disciple and making disciples in the twenty-first century.

Our hope is that this book will help you to

1. **discover** the centrality of discipleship to God's plan for your life and ministry;
2. **define** and truly understand biblical terms such as *disciple* and *go therefore and make disciples of all nations*;
3. **determine** how to get started making disciples;
4. **consider** the importance of discipleship in the context of the local church;
5. **learn** how to worship and why worship is the spiritual birthright of all disciples;
6. **gain** some practical assessment tools to help you mark progress; and
7. **enjoy** personal stories that help these principles come to life in a real way.

Is This Book for You?

Perhaps you're burning to change the world.

Perhaps you yearn to be part of something heroic, exciting, global, and eternal—to experience the very power of God by pleasing the very heart of God.

Perhaps you are trying to discover and develop a life that counts for Christ and a fruitful, satisfying personal ministry to family, friends, and colleagues.

Maybe you're part of a small, struggling congregation. Or maybe you're part of the explosive growth of "seeker churches" in North and South America. Perhaps you're planting new churches in India, Pakistan, and central Asia. Or taking the gospel deep into sub-Saharan Africa. Or leading secret Bible studies of new believers inside Communist China or East Asia. Or pastoring clandestine Middle Eastern house churches in the shadow of Islamic minarets. Or raising up teams of new lay ministry leaders in Russia. Or training new waves of young evangelists to spread out across Europe.

Perhaps you are among the many who are reading this book because you feel discouraged by how little it seems God is doing in and through your life and ministry.

Or perhaps you're reading this book because you feel overwhelmed—stressed out or burned-out—by the never-ending burdens of ministry. Perhaps you feel as though you're always responding to the myriad of human needs rather than building something solid and real and lasting and satisfying.

Whatever your unique situation, please read on—but be ready.

This book will change the way you think, the way you live, the way you do ministry. For some, it may be a radical change. For others, it may be a subtle pivot, a small but incredibly significant adjustment in your view of faith and ministry. But once you realize that God's heart breaks when his people feverishly pursue all forms of ministry strategies, projects, and tactics but fail to understand, much less obey, Christ's holy vision of spiritual investing, you *will* change.

It's time to understand *why* Jesus wants us to go "make disciples of all nations." It's time to experience the deep sense of satisfaction, contentment, and joy that comes from obeying the Lord's command to build vibrant, unified, caring communities of passionate new disciples. Indeed, it's time to discover the Spirit-filled peace that passes all understanding when we learn to do more by doing less and doing it better—when we learn to slow down, set priorities, and invest our time, talent, and treasure in the spiritual development of a few reliable people who will be qualified to invest in others.

That said, there is one important catch: the price of being discipled and of making disciples is very, very high. As Dietrich Bonhoeffer pointed out in his classic book *The Cost of Discipleship*, "When Christ calls a man, he bids him come and die." The Lord demands nothing less than our very lives. Jesus isn't looking for fans. He's looking for followers, and he expects a lot more than most people are willing to give.

Consider the following important truths from the Bible:

- To truly live, you must die (see Matthew 16:25; Luke 17:33; John 12:24).
- To truly gain, you must lose (see Matthew 10:39; John 12:25).
- To truly receive, you must give (see Matthew 10:40-42; Luke 6:38).
- To truly lead, you must serve (see Matthew 20:25-28; John 12:26).

No wonder the road to heaven is described as narrow. No wonder so few men and women are willing to become true disciples of the Lord Jesus Christ. Because the price tag can look so daunting. Yes, God's grace and salvation are free. But the journey from salvation to the finish line at the end of time is far from easy. Discipleship requires us to surrender all and be radically remade in the image of Christ.

Yet with so great a cost comes an incredibly great reward: unspeakable joy—the deepest, fullest, richest joy imaginable.

"For the joy set before Him," we read in Hebrews 12:2-3, the Lord Jesus "endured the cross, despising the shame, and has sat down at the right hand of the throne of God." Therefore, "consider Him who has endured such hostility by sinners against Himself, so that you will not grow weary and lose heart."

The Oxford American Dictionary defines *joy* as "a deep emotion of pleasure." The New Testament Greek word most often translated "joy" in English is *chara*, meaning "cheerfulness, calm delight, gladness." Are you experiencing "cheerfulness" and "calm delight" in your walk with Christ—a sense of deep contentment, a sense of fulfillment and satisfaction of a job well done, a sense that God is pleased with you, that you are safe and warm and special under the shadow of his wings?

Jesus said to his disciples, "Follow me." He may not lead you where you want to go. It may seem he leads you through hell on the way to heaven. Indeed, he may ask you to sacrifice everything dear to your heart in return for hearing at the end of your life the most thrilling twenty-nine words you can imagine:

> Well done, good and faithful servant! You have been
> faithful with a few things; I will put you in charge of
> many things. Come and share your master's happiness!
> (MATTHEW 25:21, NIV)

Are you willing to follow the Lord Jesus at all costs, to be discipled, and to make disciples of all nations?

Then, please, by all means, read on. This book is just for you.

QUESTIONS

1. Look up the following passages. What do you learn about the character and power of God?
   - Genesis 1–2
   - Luke 9:10-17
   - John 2:1-11
   - John 3:3-8
   - Ephesians 2:12-13, 19

2. Look up the following passages. Fill in the blanks and then describe in your own words—based on the Scriptures—God's purposes for believers in Christ.
   - The _____ life (John 10:10)
   - The _____ life (Romans 1:13; Galatians 5:22-23; Colossians 1:6; 1 Corinthians 16:15)
   - The _____ life (Matthew 25:14-30; Luke 19:12-27)

3. Let's consider the "invested life" more closely.
   - What spiritual gifts has God invested in you?
   - What natural talents has God invested in you?
   - How are you developing those gifts and talents?

4. How would you describe the difference between Christians (Acts 11:26) and disciples (Matthew 28:18-20; John 15:8)?

5. What are your answers to the "two simple questions" of chapter 1?
   - Who is investing in you, including those who invested in you in the past?
   - Whom are you investing in?

6. What are your needs in terms of learning discipleship? What are the costs you face for living the invested life?

7. Consider the testimony of the Haywards (starting on the next page). What was Edith Hayward's dream? What dream is God stirring in your heart?

TESTIMONY: JOHN AND EDITH HAYWARD

John and Edith Hayward.

Ever heard of them? Probably not. But their story is remarkable.

In December 1929—just about the time Wall Street was crashing and the world was beginning to slide into a terrible financial depression—this unassuming Canadian couple made an investment. And it paid off big.

The Haywards were asked by a friend to take a young man from India under their wings. They prayed about it, and by God's grace and at his direction, they agreed. The man's name was Bakht Singh. He was an engineering student, raised a Sikh, and miraculously had just trusted Christ as his personal Savior and Lord. A couple who loved the Lord with all their hearts, the Haywards asked Singh to live with them, despite the financial strain of the Great Depression. He did for the next three years.

Little did the Haywards know what they were embarking upon. Those three years proved absolutely crucial in Bakht Singh's spiritual and personal development. The Haywards showed him the love and warmth and nurturing of a close Christian family. They had meals together and studied Scripture together and prayed together, and they answered his many questions. They modeled biblical hospitality, welcoming missionaries and other believers into their home for meals and visits.

Even the Haywards' two preteen children—a boy and a girl—helped Singh grow closer to the Lord as he watched the way the children faithfully prayed during family prayer time, particularly for the urgent needs of missionaries doing the Lord's work around the world. The Lord used the Haywards to teach Singh many valuable lessons during those years, particularly the importance of intercessory prayer and finding God's will before making any crucial decisions.

Once, for example, Bakht Singh was invited to share his testimony at a Christian meeting. Without praying or seeking the Lord's will, he immediately accepted the invitation. When the Haywards learned of his hasty decision, they told Singh that he should have prayed and asked the Lord's direction before responding. Singh got angry with them for questioning his judgment.

For the next few weeks, he wouldn't even greet them when entering or leaving their home because he felt so offended. But in time, the Lord broke through and convicted Bakht Singh that a true disciple doesn't make his own plans. Instead, he seeks the Lord's will in every decision, small and large, and follows the Lord as he leads, guides, and directs. It was an important lesson for Singh, one that would mark his life and ministry forever.

Eventually it was time for Bakht Singh to return home to India. As he did, he asked God to use him to touch his fellow countrymen with the love of Christ. And God answered his prayer. Over the course of the next seven decades, Singh went on to become the greatest Christian evangelist, disciple maker, and church planter in the history of India, preaching the gospel of Jesus Christ to millions and igniting a spiritual revolution that continues to this day.

Upon his death in September 2000, *Christianity Today* noted that during his life, this Sikh convert "initiated over 6,000 indigenous churches and fellowships in India. Today his influence has seen . . . churches planted in India, Pakistan, Sri Lanka, Australia, and the United States. Singh's Bible training center, the Hebron Assembly, continues to equip hundreds of people in sharing their faith."[1] And it all started when a Christian couple obeyed Jesus' command to "go and make disciples of all nations."

Now here's the rest of the story.

Edith Hayward's dream in life was to go to India as a missionary. But the Lord had other plans for her. She married John, had children, and ministered faithfully to those in her community in Winnipeg, Canada. The Lord never gave her the opportunity to go to the country she longed to reach for Christ.

Yet by opening her home to an unknown, lonely international student and working with her husband to invest

---

[1] Corrie Cutrer, "Thousands Mourn Death of 'India's Father,'" *Christianity Today*, September 18, 2000.

in that student's spiritual growth, she helped prepare a man who would go on to bear more spiritual fruit than any other Indian in history. Of course, she didn't realize what was happening at the time. Nor could she imagine how her family's investment would pay off as God anointed Bakht Singh and used him so mightily. But what a wonderful testimony and what a wonderful model for us.

By faithfully doing something small and doing it well, John and Edith Hayward did something big. By investing in just one, they blessed many—and helped change the spiritual destiny of millions.

CHAPTER TWO

DEFINING DISCIPLESHIP

*The things which you have heard from me in
the presence of many witnesses, entrust these to
faithful men who will be able to teach others also.*
THE APOSTLE PAUL (2 TIMOTHY 2:2)

How do you become a great surgeon? Not just by going to medical school and getting the proper degrees but also by working with a senior surgeon, scrubbing in with him and seeing how he cares for people.

How do you become a great runner? Not by reading books and taking classes but by working with a great coach who will train, correct, challenge, and encourage you—a coach who will demand more than you knew was within you.

How do you become a great parent? Not simply by having children but also by having great parents who modeled lives worth emulating or by finding great parents whom you can befriend and observe and whose example you can follow.

The same is true with the Christian life.

The biblical model is that older, wiser believers take us under their wings and teach us how to follow Christ regardless of the challenges, the obstacles, and the opposition that lie ahead. Then, through time and trial and error and God's grace, we too can become older and wiser believers who can model the life and ministry of Jesus Christ for those who are younger than we are.

The key is to understand the model he gave us as our Physician, Coach, and Father. This begins with understanding God's approach to reaching the world. Yes, Jesus communicated to the masses. Yes, he preached the good news of the Kingdom to the many. Yes, he met the desperate needs of the crowds. But he discipled just a few.

For reasons that are at times obvious and at times obscure, the Father gave the Son a powerful approach for advancing his Kingdom, an approach centered on discipleship. Let's consider some of the elements of this approach that the Father evidently instructed the Son to carry out:

- I will give you twelve uneducated, unrefined men whom you will care for like family and train to change the world.
- Ask them to follow you wherever you lead them.
- Love them as individuals and build them as a team.
- Walk with them and talk with them.
- Sing with them.
- Cook with them.
- Care for their families (even their mothers-in-law).
- Spend time with their friends.

- Take them on a journey.
- Make them part of something heroic, supernatural, larger than life, and worthy of their very lives.
- Let them see you preach to the masses.
- Let them see you care for individuals.
- Let them experience fear.
- Let them experience me.
- Demonstrate to them my awesome, fearsome power.
- Challenge the way they think.
- Challenge the shallowness of their faith.
- Show them that they can't accomplish anything of lasting value through their own cleverness or strength or savvy strategies.
- Teach them to know me and follow me whole-heartedly.
- Teach them to practice my presence.
- Help them discover my power and my greatness and my majesty.
- Give them projects and assignments to test the content of their character and the quality of their faith.
- Forgive them when they make mistakes, when they fail you.
- Don't be discouraged by their shortcomings and failures.
- Understand that they won't get all this quickly or easily.
- Understand that if I don't send the Holy Spirit to help them, they won't understand who I am or be able to do anything of lasting value.
- Be patient with them.

- Use the power of your own example.
- Show them how to live by dying, how to receive by giving, how to gain by losing, and how to lead by serving.
- Show them how to care for those who are hurting.
- Show them how to excel at a few things rather than being worried and bothered and distracted by so many things.
- Show them how to live supernatural, miraculous lives.
- And all the while, teach them to teach others to teach still others.

There was another thing the Father seemed to say to his Son: "I will give you a traitor to live in your midst and turn against you. In part, this will be to fulfill prophecy and help you bring salvation to the world. But in part it will also be a lesson to those who follow in your footsteps so they won't be surprised by the fiery trials that come their way."

Let's face it: Christians are engaged in a war—a spiritual war, a global war, a "hot" war. There will be casualties. It's not your fault. It's just a painful fact of life.

A surgeon cannot save every patient.

A coach cannot run the race for his team.

A parent cannot persuade every child to be grateful and loving and obedient and productive.

But if we faithfully invest in the team God has chosen for us—following Jesus' example and key biblical principles—most of our team will go on to bear much fruit, perhaps thirty-, sixty-, or a hundredfold.

Discipleship throughout Scripture

Jesus, of course, was not the first person in history to make disciples. By doing so, he was simply following his Father's instructions and the example of the Scriptures.

Consider Moses. Yes, God spoke to Moses in direct, supernatural ways. But the Old Testament prophet also had an older, wiser man investing in his life—his father-in-law, Jethro, "the priest of Midian" (Exodus 2:16–4:18). It was Jethro who welcomed this young Egyptian exile into his family. It was Jethro who gave Moses his daughter in marriage and surely counseled and encouraged him, particularly as the Lord began to reveal himself to Moses. When God told Moses to go back to Egypt, it was Jethro who said, "Go in peace."

Later, it was Jethro who helped teach Moses how to lead the people of Israel more effectively. How? By encouraging Moses to select and train multiple layers of leaders who could share his burden of caring for people and help everyone avoid burnout. Jethro told Moses, "Select out of all the people able men who fear God, men of truth, those who hate dishonest gain; and you shall place these over them as leaders of thousands, of hundreds, of fifties and of tens. . . . So it will be easier for you, and they will bear the burden with you" (Exodus 18:21-22).

Or consider Joshua. He was discipled by Moses, followed in his footsteps, and became a great prophet and general and leader of the Israelite people.

How about the prophet Elisha? He was discipled by his predecessor, Elijah, following him, learning from him, and in turn becoming a mighty prophet of God.

Remember Andrew, Simon Peter's brother? He was a disciple of John the Baptist (John 1:35-41). Then Andrew became a disciple of Jesus and persuaded his brother to follow the Lord. Simon Peter, of course, went on to become the rock upon which Christ built his church. He heard the Great Commission, obeyed it, won men to Christ, discipled them, and taught them to disciple others. "The word of God kept on spreading; and the number of the disciples continued to increase greatly in Jerusalem, and a great many of the priests were becoming obedient to the faith" (Acts 6:7; see also Peter's two epistles).

Among those who came to faith and grew under the teaching and ministry of Peter and the other apostles was a man the disciples called Barnabas, the "Son of Encouragement." Barnabas, in turn, took men like Paul and John Mark under his wing, investing in them, helping them to develop their spiritual gifts, and encouraging them to stay the course, even when life got difficult.

John Mark went on to write the Gospel of Mark, helping people throughout history understand the life of Christ as a model for us all to follow.

Paul went on to disciple Timothy and Titus, among many others. He invested in them, took them on mission trips, and trained them to be pastors of new, growing, and challenging congregations. Paul also went on to write much of the New Testament, helping people throughout history know Christ and understand personal discipleship.

Aquila and Priscilla—coworkers with Paul and leaders of a church that met in their home—took a young believer named Apollos under their wings "and explained to him the way of God more accurately." Apollos, in turn, became a mighty evangelist, boldly spreading the gospel throughout the world against severe odds (Acts 18:18-28).

This is the pattern throughout Scripture, the pattern Paul described in 2 Timothy 2:2—"The things which you have heard from me in the presence of many witnesses, entrust these to faithful men who will be able to teach others also."

Now here's a question: How many generations of disciples does Paul refer to in this one sentence?

That's right—four.

1. **Paul** was the disciple maker—"The things which you have heard from *me* . . ."
2. **Timothy** was the disciple—"The things which *you* have heard . . ."
3. **Faithful men** were to be discipled by Timothy— ". . . entrust these to *faithful men* . . ."
4. **Other believers** were then to be discipled by these faithful men—". . . who will be able to teach *others* also."

We'll look at these elements more closely in a later chapter. The key here is to see a core principle of biblical discipleship: the principle of spiritual reproduction.

It is not enough just to be a branch of the vine. We must abide in Christ and become a branch that bears fruit.

It is not enough just to be a tree. We must be planted by streams of living water and send our roots down deep in the Word of God and become a tree that bears fruit.

It is not enough just to have God entrust us with talents.

We must invest those talents and multiply the return on God's spiritual capital.

It is not enough just to be spiritual *adults*. We must become spiritual *parents*, helping newly born-again believers grow from infancy to adulthood in Christ to the point where they, too, are able and willing to reproduce spiritually.

Is parenthood easy or painless? Of course not. "Whenever a woman is in labor she has pain, because her hour has come," Jesus said. "But when she gives birth to the child, she no longer remembers the anguish because of the joy that a child has been born into the world" (John 16:21). So, too, with spiritual parenting. The process isn't easy, but it is filled with joy.

Just as God told Adam and Eve to "be fruitful and multiply" so that the whole world would be filled with his creations (Genesis 1:28), today God is telling us to be spiritually fruitful and multiply so that the whole world will be filled with his new creations. As Jesus told his followers, "My Father is glorified by this, that you bear much fruit, and so prove to be My disciples" (John 15:8).

Three Characteristics of a Disciple

Now that we see the principle of discipleship etched on page after page in Scripture, what is a "disciple" anyway? In the pages ahead, we will explain the concept in detail. But for now, let's focus on three key, foundational points.

- A true disciple is a person who actively seeks a personal relationship with Jesus Christ and has a passionate

commitment to know him, love him, follow him, and obey his Word, no matter what the cost.
- A true disciple is a person who actively seeks a personal relationship with an older, wiser believer—someone who loves Christ and can help him grow to maturity in the Lord and develop his spiritual gifts.
- A true disciple is a person who actively seeks a personal relationship with younger believers in whose lives he, too, can spiritually invest.

Dr. Howard Hendricks of Dallas Theological Seminary put it this way:

As a follower of Jesus Christ, you need:

- a "**Paul**"—an older and wiser believer to invest in your spiritual growth;
- a "**Barnabas**"—a friend who encourages you, teaches you, and keeps you accountable; and
- a "**Timothy**"—a younger believer in whose life you can invest.[2]

A Personal Relationship with Jesus Christ

First and foremost, a true disciple continually seeks a personal relationship with Jesus Christ. A true disciple knows that God loves him. He has willingly repented (turned away) from his own sinful life and has asked God to save him and give him a new life. He has also, as Paul writes in Romans 10:9, confessed with his mouth that Jesus is Lord and has believed in his heart that God raised Jesus from the

---

[2]Howard Hendricks and William Hendricks, *As Iron Sharpens Iron* (Chicago: Moody Press, 1995) 78.

dead. According to John 3, he was thus "born again" and is part of the family and Kingdom of God.

However, while all disciples are believers, not all believers are true disciples. There is far more to being a true disciple than one's initial acceptance of Christ.

A true disciple understands the greatness of his great God. He is not merely a believer; he's a follower. He is not merely a hearer of God's Word; he is a doer of God's Word. He doesn't merely say he loves the Lord Jesus; he demonstrates his love, faith, and trust by doing whatever the Lord asks of him. His walk with God, therefore, is increasingly deep and rich and fruitful and filled with joy.

What are the two greatest commandments that Jesus explained in Matthew 22:36-40 and Mark 12:29-31? First, that we love the Lord our God with all our heart, soul, mind, and strength. Second, that we love others as ourselves.

The essence of true discipleship is supreme love and devotion to God the Father and the Lord Jesus Christ. What God desires—and what he is worthy of—is love so pure and so true that

- at all times and in all circumstances we put him first;
- at times it might even appear to some that we somehow despise our parents, our relatives, and our friends in comparison to our overwhelming and wholly devoted commitment to obeying the Father;
- we are willing to bear shame (as Christ bore the cross) for his name;

- we are willing to give up everything—even sell our most prized possessions—if he tells us to; and
- we are even willing to die, if necessary, to honor and obey him.

Consider just a few of the things Jesus said about this kind of love:

- "If you love Me, you will keep My commandments" (John 14:15).
- "If anyone comes to Me, and does not hate his own father and mother and wife and children and brothers and sisters, yes, and even his own life, he cannot be My disciple" (Luke 14:26).
- "Whoever does not carry his own cross and come after Me cannot be My disciple" (Luke 14:27).
- "None of you can be My disciple who does not give up all his own possessions" (Luke 14:33).

The question then is, how are we supposed to learn and practice such supreme love and devotion?

Our first teacher, of course, is the Word of God, for in the Word we see the life of the supreme model, the Lord Jesus Christ. Yet, by teaching us the importance of discipleship, Jesus stresses the importance of people seeing love at work in the lives of others who are ahead of us in the faith. We need to see practical, personal examples of older believers walking with Christ and integrating the Word of God into every area of their lives each and every day. Then we can better understand how we're supposed to put the Lord first in our own lives. That brings us to point number two.

A Relationship with an Older, Wiser Believer

Second, a true disciple actively seeks a personal relationship with an older, wiser believer who loves Christ and can help him grow to maturity in the Lord and develop his spiritual gifts. Simply put, a true disciple can quickly and easily answer the question "Who is investing in me?"

The Oxford American Dictionary defines *disciple* as "a person who follows the teachings of another, whom he accepts as a leader." For a secular definition, that's a pretty good start. But let's go a little bit deeper.

The Greek noun for *disciple* in the New Testament is *mathetes*. According to Greek Bible scholar Spiros Zodhiates, editor of the *Hebrew-Greek Key Word Study Bible*, the word *mathetes* "means more than mere pupil or learner. It means an adherer who accepts the instruction given to him and makes it his rule of conduct."[3] In other words, a disciple isn't someone simply jotting down notes in a Bible study or on Sunday morning. A disciple is a person who is intentionally, purposefully following the life and conduct of someone older and wiser in the faith. A disciple is a person learning by example.

Mathetes comes from the Greek verb *matheteuo*, which means to make a disciple or a follower of another's doctrine, "to instruct with the purpose of making a disciple." Zodhiates notes that "*matheteuo* must be distinguished from the verb *matheo*, which is not found in the New Testament and which simply means to learn without any attachment to

3Spiros Zodhiates, editor, *Hebrew-Greek Key Word Study Bible*, s.v. *mathetes*.

the teacher who teaches. *Matheteuo* means not only to learn but to become attached to one's teacher and to become his follower in doctrine and conduct of life."

Did you just catch the two key concepts related to discipleship? The first is that a disciple is learning to be a follower of someone's life and doctrine. The second is that a disciple has a personal attachment to his leader, his discipler. These are subtle but critical scriptural points.

Consider these examples of following and attachment from Scripture:

- **Jesus followed the Father.** "Truly, truly, I say to you, the Son can do nothing of Himself, unless it is something He sees the Father doing; for whatever the Father does, these things the Son also does in like manner" (John 5:19).
- **Jesus told his disciples, "Follow Me"** (Matthew 9:9; John 1:43).
- **The apostle Paul told his disciples to follow him.** "Follow my example, as I follow the example of Christ" (1 Corinthians 11:1, NIV)
- **Paul told Timothy to teach others to follow him.** "Show yourself an example of those who believe. . . . Take pains with these things; be absorbed in them, so that your progress will be evident to all" (1 Timothy 4:12, 15).

Obviously, you must be wise about whom you follow, something we will discuss more in the next chapter. You should never place yourself under the teaching or leadership of anyone who isn't helping you know Christ better, love him more deeply, and serve him more faithfully. Moreover, you're not seeking to become a disciple of any man or woman. You're seeking to become a more fully devoted disciple of the Lord Jesus himself. So watch your step.

That said, the scriptural model is clear: you need an older, wiser, biblically sound believer investing in your spiritual growth and personal maturity, and if you're a true disciple, you will actively seek such a relationship.

Relationships with Younger Believers

Third, a true disciple actively seeks personal relationships with younger believers in whose lives he, too, can spiritually invest. He can quickly and easily answer the question "Whom am I investing in?" He can point to specific people who meet with him on a regular basis, people who are traveling with him on their spiritual journeys and who look to him for advice, accountability, and mentoring.

This principle of spiritual reproduction—what some call the "ministry of multiplication"—is an absolutely essential element of true discipleship. Yet far too few churches put enough emphasis on it. It's not enough to grow closer to Christ or even to have someone invest in your life. You must take a risk and take others under your wing. You must invest your time, talent, and treasure in the lives of others in order to one day hear from the Father's lips, "Well done, good and faithful servant."

A disciple is a follower. A disciple maker is a leader. The best way to lead people is to inspire their trust, confidence, and respect. Are you the real thing, or are you a phony? If you're the real thing, people will want to follow and emulate you. But for them to really know if you're the real thing, you're going to need to develop a close enough relationship that they can see your faith and life and love in action, up close and personal. Then, as a person develops a personal attachment to you—in some ways similar to a father-son or mother-daughter relationship (see 1 Thessalonians 2)—that person will not only hear what you say but begin to do what you do.

This is hard for many Christians. They feel too busy or too important or too shy or too imperfect to let younger believers see and imitate their example. But there is simply no other way. You cannot disciple by remote control. You cannot disciple effectively simply by e-mail or phone or over the Internet, though these can be helpful tools, of course. Nor can you disciple simply by teaching a class or leading a Bible study.

Discipling a person involves more than just giving him information or teaching him a specific skill. The discipler-disciple relationship is different from a typical teacher-student relationship. It's more personal, more practical, and more powerful.

- A teacher shares information. A discipler shares his life.
- A teacher aims for the head. A discipler aims for the heart.
- A teacher measures knowledge. A discipler measures faith.
- A teacher is an authority. A discipler is a servant.
- A teacher says, "Listen to me." A discipler says, "Follow me."

Whom, then, are you investing in?

"I'm a pastor," you say. "I'm teaching the Scriptures to an entire congregation. I've got a staff that I manage and direct in their individual ministries."

Or "I teach a Sunday school class of twelve junior high school kids. We're studying the Acts of the Apostles. I'm teaching them the stories of the early church."

Or "I teach a Bible study group in my home. We're studying the Word, having fellowship, and praying for one another's needs."

That's great. Such teaching is very important; it's a spiritual gift essential to the growth of the church. But in and of itself, teaching is not necessarily the same as effectively "making disciples" according to the New Testament model.

Jesus was a teacher too, of course. He taught the masses. But notice that he was far more than a teacher. He also personally led a small group of men in a deeper, more personal way. They followed him. They were personally attached to him. This is the model we too must follow.

Essential Understanding

Now here's a critical point: the disciples knew Jesus was the Master, and they knew they were the apprentices. They didn't just *happen* to be hanging around him. Jesus didn't just *happen* to be spending a little more time with them than with others. That's key.

A disciple must know that he's a disciple of the Lord Jesus Christ, and he must understand that his discipler's role is to help him become more Christlike.

He can't just *happen* to be a member of your staff or Sunday school class or Bible study and thus automatically be considered a disciple in your mind. He must understand—because you've discussed it with him personally and intentionally—that you want to take him to a deeper level and that you are willing to give him special attention and instruction. He must willingly and eagerly accept the biblical model of the master-apprentice relationship. And he should feel that he's being personally invested in and is part of a team, doing something of eternal significance, something that with time and training he can model for others.

This master-apprentice relationship is woefully absent from the Western church today. Highly individualistic Westerners often focus on imparting knowledge and training the intellect, whereas Easterners tend to focus on imparting wisdom and training the will. The Western church tends to prize seminary degrees, evangelistic crusades, and large "seeker" churches.

Western ministry leaders tend to exalt the "big" and "corporate" gifts of teaching and preaching to large numbers over the seemingly "small" and "personal" gifts of shepherding and discernment and exhortation to individuals and small groups. Eastern church leaders, by contrast, in many cases have less access to seminary and such formal and exhaustive biblical training.

Thus, while Eastern church leaders certainly communicate the gospel to mass audiences as often as possible, they also tend to carefully focus on training disciples to become disciplers who will train still more disciples. That's not to say all Western churches are doing ministry wrong, and all

Eastern churches are doing it right. But we can and should learn from one another.

A healthy church needs balance. So do healthy church leaders. We certainly must be able to preach effectively to the masses with regard to the gospel and eternal life. But we must also be able to build effective master-apprentice relationships with regard to discipleship and the invested life.

Missing the Trees for the Forest

You are, no doubt, familiar with the expression "Don't miss the forest for the trees." It reminds people not to get myopic, not to get so focused on the small things in life that we miss the big picture. It's a wise saying, as far as it goes. But one could also make the case that too many pastors and church leaders today are missing the *trees* for the *forest.* They are so focused on the big picture—on reaching their communities and the world with the gospel of Jesus Christ—that they have missed the immense importance the Lord puts on the little picture, on how to care for and nurture individual "trees" until they truly bear fruit that will last.

How about you? Are you missing the trees for the forest?

"Why do you call Me, 'Lord, Lord,' and do not do what I say?" Jesus asks in Luke 6:46. In John 13:17, the Lord says, "Now that you know these things, you will be blessed if you do them" (NIV).

Many have read the words of the Great Commission that we are to go and "make disciples." But too few really understand that verse or obey it. Too few have ever been discipled. In turn, those who have not been discipled find it difficult if not impossible to disciple others. So the exact opposite of spiritual reproduction—spiritual barrenness—occurs.

Look at what has happened to the church in the Middle East, particularly in Israel and the surrounding countries, such as Turkey. These were the birthplaces of the global spiritual revolution known as Christianity. Yet after nearly two thousand years, they became among the most spiritually barren places on the face of the planet. (The good news is that the number of Jewish and Arab believers in Jesus in Israel has begun to climb steadily in the past few decades.) The seven churches of the book of Revelation are now completely extinct, good for archaeology and tourism but little else. Why is this? The reason is simple but tragic: too many of the church leaders in the Middle East utterly failed to obey the Great Commission's directive to "make disciples," to build spiritual successors capable of standing firm for Christ and advancing his Kingdom amid intense opposition. One generation of Christians failed the next. Fortunately, God in his great mercy is beginning to bring about a revival in the Middle East, and this will accelerate as we get closer to the second coming of Christ, but there are sobering lessons from the mistakes of the past two millennia.

What about where you live? Is an older, wiser spiritual generation passing on its legacy, its heritage, to the next generation? Is the local church leadership building strong disciples with deep roots able to withstand spiritual firestorms? Or when the sun comes up and the temperature heats up, will we find that the vast majority of believers dry up and wither away because their roots are shallow and their faith is weak?

Consider a brilliant, gifted leader who leads many to Christ and pastors a large church. What if he does not personally and consistently help his younger pastors and staff and lay leaders develop their spiritual gifts and become prepared to carry on the work before he dies? All the spiritual giftedness and brilliance that God has invested in him will die with him. What a tragic loss for the Kingdom of God.

What will that pastor hear from Jesus' lips if, after a lifetime of preaching and teaching and evangelism, he never fully obeyed the Great Commission to go and make disciples—not just followers of Christ but true spiritual investors who embrace the ministry of multiplication? Will he hear from the Lord's lips, "Well done, good and faithful servant"?

Only God knows for sure. But that very question should give us all pause and drive us to our knees to ask the Lord to teach us how to make disciples of all nations. If Christ said it, should we not obey it?

Ironically, a pastor who is so blessed and so gifted as a teacher and preacher can find himself so busy speaking to large groups that he never makes the time to invest in a small group of disciples. But just because a person has the spiritual gift of preaching or teaching or evangelism doesn't mean he is allowed to forget to obey the heart of the Great Commission. In addition to preaching to the masses, he must also make disciples. Jesus did both, after all. If we truly love the Master, we must follow his example.

QUESTIONS

1. Look up the following passages. What patterns do you see emerge in terms of biblical discipleship?
   - Exodus 2:16–4:18
   - Exodus 18:5-24
   - Deuteronomy 34:9
   - Joshua 1
   - 1 Kings 19
   - John 1:35-42
   - Acts 9:18-30

2. Look at Paul's words in 2 Timothy 2:2. To how many generations of disciples does Paul refer? What makes this so important?

3. What's the difference between being a spiritual adult and a spiritual parent? What biblical qualities are necessary to be a good spiritual parent?

4. A true disciple is a person who actively seeks three things. What are they?

5. "All disciples are believers, but not all believers are true disciples." What does this mean? Why is it important?

6. Look up the following verses. What's the central element of being a true disciple?
   - John 5:19
   - John 1:43
   - Matthew 9:9
   - 1 Corinthians 11:1
   - 1 Timothy 4:12, 15

7. Describe the difference between being a teacher and being a disciple maker.

TESTIMONY:
DR. T. E. KOSHY

Every disciple has a story. Mine begins deep in the heart of India.

It was there, in the state of Kerala, that I was born and raised and came to Christ at the age of ten through the love and witness of my mother. It was there, in the 1950s, that I became involved in student ministry as an undergraduate and law student at the University of Bombay, helping establish the city's first InterVarsity Christian Fellowship chapter. It was there I discovered that God is a prayer-hearing and a prayer-answering God, a God who loves us and gave himself for us. And it was there that I began to understand the power of discipleship to transform a man and mark his destiny.

The India of my youth was a land of great spiritual darkness, a land of nearly half a billion needs—cruel poverty and bitter pain, hunger and hopelessness, revolutionary fervor and great tension. It was a land where larger-than-life men waged intense ideological, political, and philosophical crusades, men like Mahatma Gandhi and Prime Minister Nehru, men who could move the masses with the power of their ideas.

But in the darkness, there was light, too. The Holy Spirit of God was also on the move in a mighty and miraculous way. My friends and I saw many come to Christ amid the dry and difficult culture of Hinduism, Muhammadanism, Buddhism, and secular nationalism. To adapt an American expression, my friends and I were "rebels with a cause," and our cause was Christ. It was not easy, but it was exhilarating.

In time, I met a "Paul," a man who was used by God to change my life forever. He did not just see me for who I was, but for who I could become. He took me under his wing and taught me how to follow Christ in a deeper, richer, more holy way. He drew me into a world where God was real and alive and powerfully present, a world where God was not an abstraction but an active force, a day-to-day reality, confronting men and offering to reshape their destinies.

That man's name was Bakht Singh. He was one of the most important evangelists and church leaders in the history of my country—indeed, in the history of the church in the twentieth century. Over the years, Bakht Singh became a friend of Billy Graham, Francis Schaeffer, Dr. Martyn Lloyd-Jones, and John Stott, among others. By the grace of God, he became my friend, spiritual father, and mentor. I was privileged to serve as one of his assistants. I worked with him, traveled with him, ate with him, listened to him, learned from him, prayed with him, and occasionally argued and disagreed with him.

When Bakht Singh died, I was asked to speak at his funeral back in India. I've never seen anything like it and probably never will again. Over the course of several days, some six hundred thousand Christians came to pay their final respects, completely shutting down the city of Hyderabad. Shops and offices were closed. Traffic was diverted. At the funeral on Friday, September 22, 2000, local officials estimated a crowd of nearly a quarter of a million. Police officers struggled in vain to control the wave of multitudes that participated in the funeral procession.

It took about three hours for the masses to cover the three kilometers from the community of Hebron—where he lived and ministered and trained disciples—to the cemetery. Indeed, it turned out to be the largest funeral procession Hyderabad had ever witnessed, as the weeping saints inched forward holding Bibles and Scripture banners, singing and praising God. It was not a typical funeral procession. It was a victory parade in honor of Christ's humble servant who had served the Lord so faithfully for some seventy years.

Bakht Singh was a household name in India when I was growing up. He was a Sikh convert, a powerful evangelist, and a remarkable church planter. He came to the village where I was growing up in Punalur, Kerala, in 1948. I can still remember his testimony, his teachings, and his compelling message. What struck me was that he was clearly a man of prayer and action and a man whom God was using mightily.

In 1953, after I graduated from high school, I attended the University of Bombay to study English literature and philosophy as an undergraduate and subsequently to earn my law degree. There I came in closer contact with Bakht Singh, especially through the ministry of a British missionary widow named Christina Durham.

Mrs. Durham was a wonderful older woman of God who ministered to university students through a ministry called the Evangelical Union. She became like a spiritual mother to me. A strong believer, she was very influential in the Indian Christian community. Her home was always open to young believers for fellowship and prayer, a good hot meal, and a listening ear. She and her late husband had founded and run a Christian publishing house in Bombay, publishing Watchman Nee's classic book *The Normal Christian Life* and many others. In fact, at one time it was one of the largest Christian publishing houses in all of Asia.

The Durhams knew Bakht Singh very well, in part because he was a trustee of the Gospel Literature Service, which they had also founded. Because of that, Bakht Singh would come to Bombay for the trustees' meetings and other ministry meetings. During the course of my studies in the mid-1950s, whenever he came to Bombay, I would meet with him. Often I would go to meetings with him. I would help him with errands or various tasks. I tried to make myself available to help him in any way I could.

Eventually he planted a church in Bombay, and I worked very closely with him, though I was still quite young. I also used to invite him to speak at various conferences and Christian camps we organized, and he graciously accepted. Over time, I had the unique opportunity to get to know him personally and see him in action up close.

In 1957, when I was twenty-four years old, Bakht Singh invited me to spend several days with him as his guest to study the Scriptures and to pray. To be invited by this renowned and revered man of God as his special guest was a tremendous honor. I quickly agreed and was very touched and impressed by what was going on in the ministry center he and his coworkers ran—the Hebron Assembly—in the city of Hyderabad.

What impressed me? Everything. For his was a life of prayer, a life of faith. While I was there, for example, I met a man named Appaji, an older man of great means. Appaji told me a story about his experience with Bakht Singh. One day Bakht Singh was praying for three thousand rupees to cover some ministry expenses. As was his way, he never told anyone about his financial needs. Instead, he prayed, trusting the Lord to provide for him. So he was praying, "Lord, you know my need."

It just so happened that Appaji had that exact amount and was taking that money to put it in the bank. But the Lord said to Appaji, "No, take it to Bakht Singh." When Appaji came and knocked on the door, Bakht Singh was still on his knees praying. So Appaji gave him the envelope and went away. Bakht Singh opened this envelope, and what did he find inside? The exact amount he was praying for.

Yes, you could say this was a "little" miracle. But the amazing thing was that the extraordinary never seemed out of the ordinary with him. It was just part and parcel of Bakht Singh's life and faith. Appaji had one story. But he was not alone. Everyone who knew this incredible Christian leader had similar stories. Miracles small and large just seemed to happen to him and around him all the time. Indeed, the early years of his ministry were marked by mighty miracles and wonders, including physical healings and great revivals. Thousands upon thousands of people, upon hearing him preach the gospel, fell to the ground and cried out for God's mercy. Once a baptismal service was apparently going to be rained out. But Bakht Singh prayed, and the rain stopped. People were baptized. The service ended. Then the rains began again.

Again, I was just twenty-four years old at the time. But I kept seeing miracles and hearing the testimonies of men and women who had experienced even greater miracles that God was doing in and through this man. And now he was taking the time to invest in me, to teach me and train me and pray with me and let me see his life and faith and incredible love and devotion to the Lord. I was so challenged and impressed because there was simply no other man of that stature and caliber in the whole of India at the time. It was like studying and working alongside the apostle Paul. Indeed, it was like being Timothy. I had found my spiritual father, and he was changing my life.

A disciple, however, does not simply get to bask in the glow of someone else's radiant faith. His own faith is tested and found wanting. That's how he grows. Whenever Bakht Singh came to Bombay, he would stay at the Durhams' home. One time he was passing through Bombay and wanted to go to the city to visit a missionary couple arriving by boat. It was a rainy day, and the buses were on strike. So Bakht Singh asked me to go outside and hail a taxi for him, even though it was rush hour and nearly impossible to get a car. I went and stood in the rain for almost an hour, as every taxi was occupied. Discouraged and disappointed, I went back and told Bakht Singh, "Brother, I am sorry; I cannot get you a taxi. It's next to impossible to get a taxi right now. It's rush hour and it's raining. Why don't you walk to the railway station? It's about a mile and a half. Then you can catch the train, go to the city, and from there you can get a taxi and meet these missionaries."

Bakht Singh wasn't bothered at all. He looked at me and said, "Well, why don't you go out again. I will go and pray."

I thought to myself, *Brother, what do you know about the situation in Bombay? I mean, what's the use of praying? This is a practical problem, not a matter of winning souls to Christ.* I didn't say any of this out loud, mind you. I just stood there kind of grumbling to myself.

In the meantime, he went into his bedroom to pray, because before Bakht Singh went anywhere, he would pray. Then he came out of his bedroom with his Bible and his briefcase. When he passed by me, I asked, "Brother, where are you going?"

"I'm going to the harbor," he replied matter-of-factly.

"How?"

"By taxi."

"Where's the taxi?"

"Well, the Lord will provide."

This I had to see. So I followed him. He walked out of the Durhams' house, out the gate, and over to the busy street. Just then a taxi came by and stopped. As two fellows got out of the taxi, Brother Bakht Singh looked back at me with a little smile, said, "That is my taxi," and got in the backseat.

I walked over to close the door for him. "Brother, your God is a great God," I said, and the taxi drove off.

This is discipleship. I was learning the greatness of our great God—that he is a prayer-hearing and prayer-answering God—by being with Bakht Singh, an older and wiser man in the faith. I could not have learned the power of prayer simply by listening to Bakht Singh or anyone else preach a sermon about prayer. I had to see it for myself. I needed a little test of my faith. I needed to see myself fail the test and see my discipler pass with flying colors in order to internalize the lesson.

CHAPTER THREE

BE DISCIPLED

By this all men will know that you are My disciples, if you have love for one another.
JESUS CHRIST (JOHN 13:35)

"Okay," you ask, "how can I find someone to invest in me?"

Great question. Allow me to make three suggestions for getting started: pray, seek, and ask.

Step One: Pray

Maybe you know you should be discipled but don't really want to be. Pray. Ask God to change your heart and give you the humility and the hunger to have someone invest in you.

Maybe you are eager to be discipled but fear you won't be able to find someone with the spiritual maturity to invest in you. Pray. God knows your heart. He can and will bring someone into your life to disciple you. If need be, he can even move someone new into your community just to disciple you, or he could move you someplace new to be discipled.

Maybe you began to be discipled once and it all went horribly wrong and you have disappointing memories. Pray. God wants you to be discipled. He has someone he wants to invest in you. And he wants it to be a positive, powerful, supernatural experience. It may seem impossible to you. But it isn't. Remember what Scripture teaches: "For nothing is impossible with God" (Luke 1:37, NLT).

Step Two: Seek

Pray daily, faithfully, and consistently. Scan the horizon. Seek to identify an older, wiser believer, someone whose life and ministry exhibit the biblical qualities you know you need to develop.

Depending on what stage of life you are in, the qualifications and maturity of the person you're looking for may differ.

Let's consider several different scenarios.

Pastors, Ministry Leaders, and Missionaries

It's lonely at the top. But it shouldn't be. That's not God's way. Nevertheless, discipleship is a tough topic for vocational ministry leaders for several reasons.

First, you may not believe you need to be discipled.

Second, you may feel embarrassed to reach out to someone for spiritual investment and encouragement. You may feel like being discipled would somehow signal weakness rather than maturity and obedience to Christ.

Third, you may think it will be too hard to find someone more mature than you who can invest in you.

All these are understandable feelings. Moreover, it may very well be true that if you're a mature believer with a deep faith and intimate walk with God, your needs are not the same as those of your staff and congregation.

That said, however, consider a few thoughts.

It is very possible that you came to Christ, grew in your faith, went to seminary or Bible school, and entered the ministry, yet *never* had anyone personally disciple you in all that time. Yes, God has taken care of you. He has taught you. He has helped you teach others. But because you have never experienced the quality and quantity of personal investment that Peter, James, John, and the other disciples experienced, you've never been gripped by the power of personal discipleship to change a person's life and destiny. You've never been fully impacted by the counterintuitive strategy of the Great Commission, that the way to reach the whole world is to invest in a small group. Since you've never been shaped by discipleship, you've never modeled discipleship.

That's understandable, but in all honesty, that's not doing God's work God's way, is it?

Have you ever given a sermon on the importance of evangelism in which you paraphrased the Great Commission from Matthew 28 as "Go into all the world and tell them the good news of salvation"? Or "Go and share the gospel with all nations"?

Well, of course, it is true that Jesus wants us to take the good news of the Kingdom into all the world. There are many verses that tell us this, verses such as Matthew 24:14 and Mark 16:15 and Acts 1:8. But in Matthew 28:18-20, Jesus specifically says we are to go and "make *disciples* of all the nations." This command is certainly based on the premise that we must be sharing the gospel with all people and helping them to repent and come to a saving knowledge of Christ. But it goes a step further and exhorts us to invest in a new generation of investors.

The emphasis of the Great Commission isn't simply on communicating the message; it's on creating new messengers.

It isn't simply about telling the many; it's about training the few.

We aren't called to simply spread the message wide; we're called to go deep.

The truth is, we all need a Paul in our lives, someone to love us and invest in us. Even pastors. *Especially* pastors.

You can't simply draw from your own spiritual, emotional, and intellectual capital all your life. It's not healthy. It's not biblical. You need to be refreshed and encouraged, developed and challenged. You need to be loved and cared for. You need someone you can relax with, ask tough questions of, laugh with, and confide in. You need someone to keep you accountable and call more out of you than you ever knew you had.

You need someone to spend time with, someone who is able to help you get a true sense of what discipleship is all about—what it should mean for your life, the lives of your staff members, and the lives of those under your care. Even though it will inevitably look different in style and substance from the discipleship relationship a younger believer might have, it is important that you be discipled for two reasons: first, for yourself, and second, to set an example for your flock. After all, how can you encourage the people under your pastoral care to make disciples if you have never been discipled and aren't making disciples? It won't work. Leaders must lead. There is no other way.

Now, then, what specifically should you do?

You might begin by prayerfully seeking out

- **Your own father or father-in-law.** If either is a godly man of faith and wisdom, don't be afraid to reach out to him and ask him to invest more time and teaching and prayer in you. Consider the powerful example of Moses' father-in-law, Jethro, in Exodus 18.
- **A retired pastor.** If you're looking for someone who has "been there, done that" and is ahead of you in years and life experience, look for a retired pastor in your area whom you know (or can get to know) and trust. If it's appropriate, you might even consider reconnecting with one of the men who once pastored the very church you now lead.
- **An older, active pastor.** A man doesn't have to be retired to be able to take you under his wing. Look for an older, wiser pastor in your own community (if you're a senior pastor or missionary) or in your own church (if you're an associate pastor or other level of ministry staff). If you're a senior pastor, you might even consider a pastor from another denomination who might be able to invest time and attention in you, so long as there are no critical theological differences that would do more harm than good.
- **A seminary professor.** If you have an excellent seminary or Bible college near you, perhaps there's

a faculty member there—or someone the dean or president or a faculty member could recommend to you—who could invest in you.

- **A missionary.** Who discipled Timothy? A missionary and church planter named Paul. Perhaps one of the missionaries your own church supports—or one who is retired or home on furlough—has the marks of a mature believer and could invest in you.
- **A church elder.** If you're a young pastor, you might seek one of the elders in your church who is older and more experienced in the faith.

The best-case scenario is finding someone who is both

- **mature**—well ahead of you in his relationship with the Lord and committed to the practice of discipleship and spiritual investment; and
- **local**—able to invest time and prayer in you up close and personally. This is particularly important for a pastor or someone in vocational ministry leadership. Life is too fast, too challenging, and too full of disappointments, discouragements, and temptations to leave your discipleship to someone far away.

If you were once discipled—back in college or seminary, perhaps—but haven't kept in touch with your discipler for some time, our suggestion would be for you to find a way to reconnect. Rekindle your relationship. Visit each other, even if it costs you time and money. Begin a correspondence like Paul had with Timothy. Don't let a good discipleship relationship wither on the vine. It's too rare, too valuable to neglect or give up on.

If after much prayer and seeking, you really can't find a Paul to take you under his wing, try to at least find a Barnabas, a mature colleague in the ministry who can be a prayer and accountability partner. Pray about taking a sabbatical or a furlough to a place where God might give you someone who can invest great quantities of quality time in you and, if you have a family, in your spouse and children. This book is a good place to start to learn about the invested life. But you need personal attention, and—precisely because you are so busy—you must make personal discipleship for yourself and your family your top priority. It is that important.

Whatever you do, don't be discouraged. God loves you. He has called you into ministry. He has brought you to this specific role. He will care for you. He will equip you. You are not alone. The Lord will provide someone to invest in you.

Lay Leaders

It is true that pastors, ministry staff, and missionaries have it tough. But you as a lay leader really have it tough. You're one of the most valuable and important assets in your church. Yet you're also one of the most overlooked groups when it comes to discipleship. People assume you have "arrived"—you're a leader, after all—so you don't need special care and attention. But as you well know, nothing could be further from the truth.

Maybe you're a Sunday school teacher or Bible study leader or youth group leader or children's ministry coordinator or in some other position of lay leadership. But maybe you've never been personally discipled. Now is the time.

Don't think that just because you are a leader you can't or shouldn't seek someone to invest in you or that you should let others younger and needier get all the attention. To the contrary. You should be at the top of the list to receive the church's time. But maybe you aren't. Too many churches invest far too little in their lay leaders. If you show just the slightest bit of spiritual giftedness, rather than invest in you and help you develop your spiritual gifts, many churches will ask you to take on some important but intense and exhausting ministry assignment, providing you little or no assistance. You might get a detailed workbook. You might be invited to an occasional leadership training seminar or various leadership retreats. But rarely will you be included in a pastor's or elder's personal Bible study or discipleship group or be regularly invited over to a pastor's or elder's home or called and e-mailed on a regular basis to see how you're doing. All too often you can feel forgotten and taken for granted.

That's not healthy. That's not how the church is supposed to work.

In addition to discipling their own ministry staff, pastors should make discipling the lay leaders in their congregations a top priority. These lay leaders may not be the "squeaky wheels" that always seem to get the grease. But they tend to have the very qualities good disciples must have: they tend to be like the "good soil" Jesus referred to in Luke 8:8 and 8:15—"these are the ones who have heard the word in an honest and good heart, and hold it fast, and bear fruit with perseverance."

Pastors: invest heavily in these folks.

They won't disappoint you. Instead, they will bear more fruit than you ever would have imagined.

Now, if you are a lay leader but no church leader has yet recognized that you need to be invested in precisely *because* you're a lay leader, don't get discouraged. Resist that temptation with all the power God will give you. Don't let yourself become burned out or cynical. Don't let yourself become a spiritual casualty.

The Father loves you. He wants to invest in you. He will never leave you nor forsake you. The Great Commission is about making disciples, but it's also about Jesus' promise that "I am with you always, even to the end of the age" (Matthew 28:20). And as Jesus said in John 14:18, "I will not leave you as orphans; I will come to you."

So prayerfully seek someone to invest in you. Start by seeing if your senior pastor has time for you. If he's already fully committed—or for any other reason is unable or unwilling to invest in you—see if one of the other pastors or ministry staff leaders could begin investing in you. What about one of your church elders or deacons? What about one of the older, more mature couples in your church? What about a local or retired or furloughed missionary? Are they willing, able, and available?

Scan the horizon. Watch. Pray. Trust that God will show you someone who can take care of you and invest in you. Again, look for someone who truly is older and more mature than you, someone who has more Christian and life experience and who is bearing the fruit of the Spirit, leading people to Christ, and helping them grow in their faith.

New Believers

If you've just recently trusted Jesus Christ as your Savior, you are probably beginning to discover just how much you need someone older and wiser to teach you the ropes and help you grow in your faith. That's good. Now it's vital that you find someone to disciple you right away.

The first person to look to for discipleship might be the person who led you to Christ. He already knows you and should have a personal interest in helping you grow.

If that person is not able or available, consider other Christians you might know who seem to display a level of spiritual maturity and have the time and willingness to invest in you.

If you accepted Christ in a worship service or through an evangelistic outreach or by reading a book or hearing a radio or TV show—or some way other than through a personal relationship with a fellow believer—then here are some practical suggestions for you to get started in your faith and find someone to disciple you:

- **Find a church home.** Begin by seeking out a local church where the Bible is preached faithfully, where people pray constantly, and where you have the opportunity to worship the God who loves you and gave himself for you. Take Communion and be baptized.
- **Take a new believers' class.** If there is a class for new believers—one that will walk you through the basics of building a personal relationship with Christ, of learning to read and study the Bible for yourself,

and of developing the spiritual disciplines of prayer,
fellowship, Communion, tithing, and so forth—join
it right away and attend faithfully.

- **Join a Sunday school class.** Once you finish a new
believers' class (or if there is no such class), find an
appropriate Sunday school class within your church
where you can learn the Bible and develop lasting
friendships and prayer partnerships with fellow
believers.
- **Join a small-group Bible study.** Seek out and join a
small-group Bible study as soon as possible, perhaps
one that is connected to your Sunday school class.
This is where true personal relationships, prayer,
accountability, and spiritual growth can begin to
take place.
- **Meet with your pastor.** Set up a meeting with your
pastor as soon as possible. Ask him if there is someone
who could teach you the basics of the faith and begin
discipling you. If the pastor himself is available, great.
Start right away. If he isn't available, ask him to direct
you to one of the elders or deacons or older couples in
the church to be discipled.
- **Pray, pray, pray for someone to disciple you
personally.** As you are obedient in finding a church
home, studying God's Word, and developing personal
relationships with other believers, keep praying
faithfully for someone specific to disciple you. God
will hear your prayer, and you'll be excited to see
him provide for you in a supernatural way. You are
not alone.

What to Look for in a Discipler

Be careful who invests in you.

You're not looking for a guru. You're looking for a model who will help you become more like Christ. If your discipler isn't truly following Christ—if he isn't becoming more and more like Christ every day—you run a very serious risk of picking up ungodly, un-Christlike characteristics, exactly opposite of your goals. Be wise in your judgment.

In Titus 1:7-9, Paul describes the qualities of character that should define an overseer, a church leader. Likewise, when seeking someone to disciple you, look for someone who is

1. **Above reproach.** No one's perfect. But is this leader a cut above? Is he pursuing a holy, pure life, careful to avoid even the appearance of evil? Or is he sloppy and in danger of harming the cause of Christ?

2. **God's steward.** Is he a good steward of the time, talent, and treasure God has invested in him, or is he a poor manager of himself and others?

3. **Not self-willed.** Does he care about others, or is he completely self-absorbed?

4. **Not quick-tempered.** Does he master his anger, or does he allow his anger to master him?

5. **Not addicted to wine.** Different churches have different views about whether drinking alcohol is acceptable. If your church finds it acceptable to drink in moderation, does this leader watch his step or does he have a drinking (or other substance abuse) problem?

6. **Not pugnacious.** Is he eager to listen to and make peace with all men as much as it is possible to do so without sacrificing basic biblical principles, or is he eager to fight and aggressive toward you and/or other members of the congregation or community?

7. **Not fond of sordid gain.** Does he set the highest possible standard with regard to his own finances and the church's finances, or are there hints of greed or cutting moral and ethical corners financially?

8. **Hospitable.** Does he (and his family, if he has one) practice biblical hospitality, regularly inviting people over to his home and letting them share in his life, or is he standoffish and distant? Does he keep an eye out to care for those who seem lonely and on the fringes of the community, or does he keep company only with the "in crowd"?

9. **Loving what is good.** Does he focus on what is good in people and encourage them to grow and excel in those areas, or is he negative and condescending, bitter and depressing?

10. **Sensible.** Does he seem mature, wise, balanced, and reasonable, or does he tend to make rash, impetuous, or unwise decisions?

11. **Just.** Does he value fairness or favoritism? Does he care for those who have been wounded by injustice, or does he seem blind to their needs and fears and concerns?

12. **Devout**. Does he seem truly devoted to building his personal relationship with the Lord, or is he more concerned with building a name for himself and a ministry empire?

13. **Self-controlled**. Does he exhibit evidence of being controlled by the Holy Spirit and demonstrating the fruit of the Spirit (Galatians 5:22-23)? Is he able to control the "lust of the flesh and the lust of the eyes and the boastful pride of life" (1 John 2:16), or does he wink at sin and find himself easily seduced by these great temptations?

14. **Holding fast the faithful Word**. Does he know how to teach God's Word? Does he know how to effectively communicate God's truths? And is he actually teaching the Word of God and not the latest whim or fad? Do you actually hear him quote and teach Scripture extensively, or does he seem more enamored of secular or quasi-spiritual stories, anecdotes, poems, and parables?

15. **Able to exhort in sound doctrine**. Does he understand how to exhort (that is, to urge, advise, encourage, and challenge earnestly) men and women to follow the teachings of Christ, prodding them forward in their faith, or does he let people hear the Word without taking action? Is he active in sharing his faith in Christ with those who are lost? Is he actually leading people into the Kingdom of God? Does he practice what he preaches?

16. **Able to refute those who contradict.** Is he
    grounded well enough in his knowledge of the
    Scriptures to counter skeptics and set them straight,
    or does he seem to possess a superficial knowledge
    of the Word and be in over his head when it comes
    to deeper theological discussions?

That's quite a list!

Again, you won't find a perfect leader to disciple you. But
you do want to be on the lookout for someone truly ahead of
you spiritually—wiser, more knowledgeable, and more faithful in following Christ than you are right now.

Consider, too, the beginning of the next chapter of Paul's
letter to Titus:

> You, however, must teach what is appropriate to
> sound doctrine. Teach the older men to be
> temperate, worthy of respect, self-controlled, and
> sound in faith, in love and in endurance. Likewise,
> teach the older women to be reverent in the way they
> live, not to be slanderers or addicted to much wine,
> but to teach what is good. Then they can urge the
> younger women to love their husbands and children,
> to be self-controlled and pure, to be busy at home,
> to be kind, and to be subject to their husbands, so
> that no one will malign the word of God. Similarly,
> encourage the young men to be self-controlled. In
> everything set them an example by doing what is
> good. In your teaching show integrity, seriousness
> and soundness of speech that cannot be condemned,

so that those who oppose you may be ashamed
because they have nothing bad to say about us.

TITUS 2:1-8 (NIV)

As a general rule, men should not be discipled by women, and women should not be discipled by men. After all, the process of discipleship is very personal and intimate. It involves growing close to a person and understanding his innermost heart, thoughts, and attitudes and letting him know yours. It involves letting Christ work in the most sensitive areas of your life to make you the person God truly wants you to be. Thus, you must be very careful not to put yourself in the way of temptation. If you are discipled by someone of the opposite sex, you run the risk of becoming romantically or sexually attracted to that person and, in turn, put yourself at grave risk of falling into sin and embarrassing the cause of Christ. Thus, Paul urges men to disciple men and women to disciple women, to keep us from temptation and sin.

Now, it is true that Scripture doesn't give us inviolable directives in this regard. Jesus ministered to women—even prostitutes—though he did not select women to be apostles. Paul ministered to and with women, though we read of no women whom he personally discipled. Thus, pastors and church leaders and men who are followers of Christ may minister to and counsel women, even disciple them, in the context of a larger group or ministry staff. But generally it would be wiser not to. Anyone who does so must fully understand, appreciate, and weigh the risks and dangers involved.

Spiritual leaders should never think of themselves as invulnerable to *physical* sexual sin (becoming sexually involved with someone to whom one is ministering) or *emotional* sexual sin (becoming romantically attached to someone to whom one is ministering). Indeed, spiritual leaders are arguably *more* vulnerable to such temptations because Satan wants to destroy these people and eliminate their usefulness in advancing God's Kingdom. All around us we see spiritual leaders falling into sexual sin, sometimes willfully, sometimes carelessly and when they least expect it.

Discipleship should never become a doorway for spiritual destruction. So we urge you to be very, very careful. Err on the side of caution at all times. Use discretion and discernment, and make sure to do all things for the edification of Christ's body and for God's eternal glory. Take Paul's advice: teach the older women to disciple the younger women. And "whether, then, you eat or drink or whatever you do, do all to the glory of God" (1 Corinthians 10:31).

All this said, if after much prayer and seeking, you still can't find someone in your church who is a mature follower of Christ to invest in you, pray about going to a church that truly understands and obeys 2 Timothy 2:2 and the ministry of discipleship and spiritual reproduction.

Step Three: Ask

Often in Scripture, older, wiser leaders approach younger believers and invite them to be discipled. Certainly the ideal situation is for someone to reach out to you. Elisha didn't ask Elijah. Peter didn't ask Jesus. Timothy didn't ask Paul.

That said, however, nothing in Scripture prohibits you from asking someone to disciple you. It is, therefore, appropriate to prayerfully approach someone and ask to be discipled. As Jesus said, "Ask, and it will be given to you; seek, and you will find; knock, and it will be opened to you. For everyone who asks receives, and he who seeks finds, and to him who knocks it will be opened" (Matthew 7:7-8). Furthermore, Jesus said, "Until now you have not asked for anything in my name. Ask and you will receive, and your joy will be complete" (John 16:24, NIV).

If you seek the heart of God in order to do the will of God, he will open a door and bring an older, wiser follower of God into your life.

Here are a few suggestions on how you might proceed with the process of asking:

1. **Pray.** Prayer cannot be overemphasized. Pray, pray, pray that God will lead the right person to you or you to the right person.

2. **Start slow.** Once you've identified a person whom you'd like to ask to disciple you, you might want to consider inviting that person over for dinner or out for a meal or a cup of coffee to get to know each other a bit better before you "officially" ask to be discipled. Break the ice. Build a personal relationship. See if the person would be willing to get together to pray with you about some specific issues. Ask him for some advice about questions that are troubling you. See if he responds warmly and wisely to you, and ask him to pray with you.

   It's much easier to go slow at the beginning—to ask only for a few specific meetings at first—and then decide this person might not be right for you (for whatever reason) than to ask a person to disciple you and then quit after a few days, weeks, or months.

3. **Ask, and be specific.** If you and the person you'd like to disciple you seem to be a good fit and are getting along well, then you may want to ask to be discipled. Be specific about what you're looking for, what your expectations are, and why you're asking this person in particular. The best place to start is to ask him to pray with you regularly. You also may want to give him a copy of this book if he's not read it so he can get a sense of where you're coming from and where you'd like to go.

4. **Set a short, specific time frame for discipleship at first.** As a general rule, we believe it's better to avoid open-ended, vague commitments. Can we offer you a scriptural basis for this? No, we can't, and thus you're welcome to disregard this advice. But you may want to consider asking someone to get together to disciple you for, say, three months at first. After the agreed-upon time, if things are going well and you both sense God is blessing the relationship, then by all means extend the terms. But if things are not going so well, it's good to know you don't have to quit but can get to the end of the agreed-upon time, kindly thank each other, and go your separate ways. Again, it's just a suggestion based on years of experience, but it's one designed to help you avoid or minimize hurt feelings and anxiety.

5. **Prayerfully set goals and come together with questions.** If you ask someone to disciple you, prayerfully work together to set specific goals about what you both want to accomplish. When you get together, come with questions you want answered. Don't let your time drift. Have a plan, stick to it, and learn as much as you possibly can from the person God has brought into your life.

6. **Learn to listen and to follow.** The danger in asking someone to disciple you instead of his asking you is that you can develop a sense that you are in charge, that you are running the show. That's why prayer and seeking the right person are so important *beforehand*. Because once someone begins to disciple you, you need to learn submission. You need to learn to follow. You need to learn to honor those who are older and wiser in the faith.

   Obviously, you shouldn't follow ungodly counsel or an ungodly model. But this should have been taken care of by the screening process of prayer and seeking. If you truly have an older, wiser believer discipling you, then we have but one piece of advice for you: *listen*. Sure, ask questions, dig deeper, express your concerns or doubts or frustrations. But listen, listen, listen. If he gives you homework, do it. If he asks you to memorize Scripture, do it. If he suggests you go to a conference or on a short-term mission trip, do it. If he raises some concern about an area of your spiritual or personal or professional life, take him seriously. Ask him for biblical and practical advice. If he believes you need to have a special meeting with a pastor or counseling professional, take his suggestion.

This is not blind obedience we're talking about. It's called following an older, wiser believer as he follows Christ. It's called learning to follow faithfully.

Now let us offer here a brief warning: don't be surprised—and don't let yourself be discouraged—if, when you're talking to your pastor or Sunday school class leader or some other leader, they don't understand or aren't interested in your desire to be discipled. In some ways, that's the whole point of this book—to help more people understand the importance of living the invested life. If, as you're reading this, you realize you want and need to be discipled, then God is stirring you to do his will his way. That's exciting. If the people you're looking to be discipled by don't see the power of this vision, then we recommend two things:

- First, keep prayerfully looking for someone who *does* understand discipleship and will take you under his wing.
- Second, keep praying faithfully for your ministry leadership. Consider giving them a copy of this book and asking for their feedback.

Don't push too hard. Just gently seek to get a discussion started about what discipleship is and the role it might play in your church down the road. Remember, as a general rule, your pastors and ministry staff are good, godly people—and very busy. It is easy for them to be overwhelmed by all the human and spiritual needs before them. It is not easy for them to get excited about or pass along something that hasn't already been part of their life experience. But our God is a great God, a prayer-hearing and a prayer-answering God, a wonder-working God. Pray for your spiritual leaders. Encourage them. Don't berate them. Seek ways to influence them and get a gentle dialogue started. Seek to serve them humbly and faithfully and without compensation. And just see what God will do in their midst and yours.

QUESTIONS

1. Have you ever had a "Paul" in your life, an older and wiser believer who took you under his wing and invested in your spiritual growth? If so, reflect back on that relationship and note what made it special and important to you. If not, what would you find valuable about such a relationship?

2. Do you have a "Barnabas" in your life—a friend who loves you, encourages you, and keeps you accountable? If so, what makes that person so valuable? If not, who are some people who could become a "Barnabas" for you?

3. What are some qualities you have that would make you a good "Timothy," someone a "Paul" would want to invest in?

4. If you have never been discipled, what are the reasons holding you back?

5. Study Titus 1:7-9. What character traits should define a church leader?

6. Is there a difference between the character that should define the life of an elder and the character that should define the life of a disciple maker? What should be the standard for the person discipling you?

7. How do you feel about the notion that "too many churches invest far too little in their lay leaders"? How is your church doing? How can your church do better in this area, if it is lacking?

8. Study Titus 2:1-8. Why should you avoid being discipled by (or discipling) someone of the opposite sex?

TESTIMONY: GANDHI

DR. T. E. KOSHY

I had great plans to become a high-powered lawyer and reach the educated elite of my country for Christ or to become a foreign correspondent and travel the world, covering the great events shaping our times.

My destiny was not—I was convinced—on the dusty, dirty, poverty-stricken streets of India. It was in receiving a world-class education and walking the halls of power in the world's most important capitals. In following my ambitions, I would go on to pursue and receive five college and university degrees and travel to Washington, D.C., as a journalist, eventually covering President Lyndon B. Johnson at the White House.

But my discipler, Brother Bakht Singh, frequently challenged me. "The only thing God is building in this world is his church," he would say. "Why write about history when you can make it? Why *spend* your life reporting about the lives of the rich and famous when you can *invest* your life helping the humble and the needy meet the God who loves them and gave himself for them? If you have no successor, are you truly a success?" Such were the questions that seemed to ring in my ears.

It took me many years to understand how I was supposed to apply the lessons I was learning from Bakht Singh to the unique plan and purpose God had for my life. For one thing, when it came to being a practicing lawyer or journalist, God made it clear to me his answer was "No." He wanted me to go to Bible college in England and prepare for the ministry. I struggled with that, but eventually I went in obedience.

While in England, some people connected with Inter-Varsity Christian Fellowship who knew I'd been discipled by Brother Bakht Singh invited me to embark on a speaking tour through all the major universities of England, including Oxford and Cambridge. I couldn't believe it.

I arrived at Oxford University to speak to a group of doctoral candidates, most of whom were not Christians. I was assigned a subject to speak on, specifically the uniqueness of Christ and the futility of philosophy. So of course, I brushed up on my reading of all the great philosophers such as Socrates, Aristotle, and Plato. I gathered quotations from all these important people and prepared a twelve-page lecture to present the next day. At midnight, I was on my knees praying, asking the Lord to bless my presentation. After all, I had seen Brother Bakht Singh pray about everything—absolutely everything—and I was seeking to follow his example. But something happened I didn't expect—and didn't like.

The Lord said to me very clearly, "Throw that lecture in the dustbin."

"What? Lord, what do you mean by that?" I asked, stunned. "Then what shall I speak about?"

"Tell them about your experience with me," the Lord said.

"Lord," I argued, "I came to know you at ten years old. I was not a murderer. I was not a drug addict. I don't have exciting stories to tell these people. Lord, don't you know? These are not Sunday school kids. They are brilliant. *This is Oxford University.*"

But the Lord said to me, "Listen, who knows better, you or me? If you know better than I do, why are you asking me to bless this lecture that you've written? If you want me to bless your talk, then tell them your experiences with me."

"Lord, you are giving me a very hard task," I said glumly.

I must confess, that night I had a real hard time with the Lord. Here I was on a speaking tour for him, but I didn't want to do God's work God's way. All night, I wrestled with what God was asking of me, my pride battling against my faith.

The next day I arrived at the lecture hall, and the chairman introduced me—very formally, as they do in England—explaining the subject I was assigned to speak on. Imagine, then, his surprise when I stood and said, a bit sheepishly, "Yes, I was going to speak on that subject. In fact, I prepared this lecture . . ." I held it up because I wanted them to know I could do better than what I was about to do. My ego at work. "But I'm not going to deliver it."

A hush settled over the crowd. My stomach was tied up in knots.

"As I was praying last night, the Lord asked me to tell you about my experiences with Jesus. Perhaps some of you may not like it," I said, having little doubt about that.

I was already seeing my Waterloo, my downfall and humiliation. *Okay,* I thought. *These fellows will never invite me back to Oxford. This is the end of it. But yes, Lord, I will obey* (however begrudgingly). I continued speaking. "So I prayed and asked the Lord, 'What do you want me to speak on?' He said, 'Christ the Savior, Christ the Sovereign, Christ the Sufficiency, Christ the Strength, Christ the Supplier, Christ the Security, and Christ the Soon-Coming King. He gave me the outline last night while I was on my knees." Then I shared from my heart how the Lord had become real to me in each of these seven ways. After speaking, I just wanted to hide myself.

When it was over, the audience clapped in their traditional, formal way. The chairman of the lecture said, very politely, "Well, thank you, Mr. Koshy, for coming and enlightening us. Now, if any of you would like to talk to him about anything further, he will be available."

Where's the door? I thought. I was sure nobody would stay.

But no one left. To my utter astonishment, not a single student left the lecture hall. Instead, each and every one of them formed a line to ask me questions. Many teared up as they shook my hand, barely controlling their emotions, and said, "Come back again; we want to hear more of this kind of lecture." I couldn't believe my eyes or ears.

Then I noticed one Indian—the only other Indian in the

entire room—standing at the end of this long line of students waiting to talk with me. I knew this young man had to be somebody important to have the education and wealth and influence to be here at Oxford University. I desperately wanted to meet him and talk with him. I was afraid the long line would discourage him and he might leave. But I couldn't exactly walk away from everyone else and go directly to this Indian. What could I do?

I began praying in my heart that the Lord would constrain this fellow to stay so I could meet him, and the Lord answered my prayers. Though it took more than half an hour before his turn came, this young Indian man came and grabbed me by the hand and said, "Sir, I want to thank you for coming and speaking on your experiences with Jesus. Ever since I came to Oxford, I have been going to churches to hear about Jesus Christ. All I have been hearing have been philosophical discourses, far removed from the realities of God."

Inside, as I listened to this enthusiastic, grateful student, I felt ashamed. For that was exactly what I was going to tell this audience. That was exactly what I had prepared. A philosophical discourse.

"But today you came," he continued. "You spoke to us from your heart about your own personal experiences with Jesus. Perhaps many may not agree with you. But no man can refute what you said."

"What is your name?" I asked him eagerly.

"My name is Ramchandran," he said.

"What is your last name?" I pressed.

"Please don't ask me that," he replied. "The moment

people hear my last name they behave as though I have no first name. I am sick and tired of that. So please don't ask me."

I asked him again, but he resisted.

"Please," I implored him. "Please."

He hesitated, but then he lowered his voice and said, "If you insist, it is Gandhi."

I was stunned, not knowing what to say.

"You are Mahatma Gandhi's grandson?"

"That is what I told you. See, now you are talking about Mahatma Gandhi. Now you are not interested in me."

I was speechless.

Here was one of the grandsons of the renowned Mahatma Gandhi, the father of India, who had led the nonviolent revolution for freedom from the British and sought, though unsuccessfully, to create a sense of harmony and unity between Hindus and Muslims. And Mahatma Gandhi was this young man's father's father. His mother's father was the last governor-general of India, who took the reins of power for India back from the British via Lord Mountbatten in 1947, when India became an independent country. Here I was speaking with— indeed, sharing the gospel of Jesus Christ with—a grandson of two of the most influential Indians of all time.

I immediately assured him that I was most definitely interested in him personally, and we continued chatting for some time. Unfortunately, however, it got late. I had to get back to my college. So I thanked Ramchandran Gandhi, and we parted ways. The secretary of the organization who invited me began driving me back to my room. He was a blue-eyed young Englishman. It was raining. I still remember that night, for as he was driving, he broke down crying.

"The moment when you got up and said that you were changing the subject and you were going to speak on your experiences with Jesus, I said to myself that I wished we had not invited you.

"But," he quickly added, trying to hold back his tears, "that message was for me. I am a Christian. I was backsliding. That message challenged my heart." He started weeping so hard he had to pull the car to the side of the road. Then he controlled himself, continued driving, and dropped me off at the railway station.

Some time later I received a letter from Oxford.

Will you consider coming and spending three
months with us to give more lectures?

That encounter provided a formative lesson for me.

As true disciples of Jesus Christ, we must always be willing to do God's work in God's way. We must be willing to go where he sends us and say what he tells us to say. We must always be ready to share our faith—always ready for "divine appointments"—because we never know who is listening.

Here I had wanted to become a great lawyer or journalist to reach the influential elites of India for Jesus. I had argued with the Lord when he said no to my own plans and strategies.

But what happened? The Lord Jesus himself took me thousands of miles away from India, to Bible college in England of all places, on a speaking tour to Oxford, just to meet and share the gospel with the grandson of Gandhi.

Our God is an awesome God.

He works in mysterious ways. The question is, will we let him work that way in our lives? Or will we rebel, thinking we know better?

Some years later, I was passing through Delhi. I picked up the phone and called the home of Dr. Gandhi. His wife answered.

"Is Dr. Gandhi available?" I asked.

"Yes," she said. "Who is this?"

I explained who I was and said that we once met at Oxford. Suddenly the young man was on the line. "Dr. Gandhi, you may not remember me. My name is Koshy."

This was thirteen years later. But you know what he said? "Are you the Koshy who came to Oxford and spoke on the subject of the uniqueness of Jesus Christ and your personal experience with him?"

"You mean you still remember that?" I asked, amazed.

"How can I ever forget it? Do you have time to have a meal with me?"

The next day he came and picked me up and took me to a restaurant in New Delhi. We had lunch. What he said humbled me. "Jesus Christ is God's ultimate incarnation. He alone could identify with the sufferings of the masses." The more we talked, the more amazed I grew, for the grandson of Mahatma Gandhi had become a believer in Jesus Christ.

In time I would obey the Lord's voice and Brother Bakht Singh's advice. By God's grace I was married, became a pastor, became the evangelical chaplain at Syracuse University in upstate New York, planted a church, and launched International Friendship Evangelism, a ministry to international students in the United States and around the world.

My passport would be filled with many stamps, but for God's glory, not my own.

For about eight months every school year at Syracuse University, my wife, Indira, and I, along with our ministry team, build bridges of relationships cross-culturally with students from all over the world. We host "friendship lunches" and other meals for them. We teach them conversational English. We invite them to picnics and other outings to help them make friends. We teach them about the love of Jesus Christ. We invite them to receive Christ as their personal Savior and Lord. And we disciple them one-on-one and in small groups, equipping them to go back to their home countries and reach their families, friends, and countrymen for Christ.

Then, for about three or four months of the year, my colleagues and I travel around the world, responding to requests from former students that we visit them, help them establish new churches, discover and share the joy of biblical worship, and teach them how to disciple others and train up new leaders. It has not been the life I envisioned for myself some four decades ago. No, it has been far more satisfying and, I pray, far more useful.

FOLLOW JESUS' MODEL

Jesus "appointed twelve, so that they would be with Him and that He could send them out to preach, and to have authority . . ."

MARK 3:14-15

Just as there is such great joy in becoming a natural parent and raising a child "in the way he should go" (Proverbs 22:6), so, too, we believe there is no greater joy in life than becoming a spiritual parent. This involves creating a warm and loving and nurturing environment and raising spiritual children into mature men and women who will then be capable of leading spiritually productive lives and becoming spiritual parents themselves.

The question then is, "How?"

Making Disciples Jesus' Way

The key to becoming a spiritual parent is following the model of the Lord Jesus Christ as found in the New Testament.

Loving God

First, as Jesus grew up, he set an example of loving God without reservation and thus became a mature man of faith and a fully devoted follower of his heavenly Father. This should be your goal too. If you're going to become an effective disciple maker—leading people into a deeper walk with God—you must first become a faithful disciple, an increasingly wise and mature follower of the Father. Remember, even Jesus—God incarnate—did not begin making disciples right away. He was willing to *follow* before he began to *lead*.

Consider some key elements of Jesus' preparation for ministry:

- Jesus had godly, faithful parents whom God used to give him birth, love him, raise him, and—to an important though limited degree—help him develop his walk with his Father in heaven (Luke 1–2).
- Jesus obeyed his parents and, in turn, obeyed his heavenly Father (Luke 2:41-51).
- Jesus kept increasing (Luke 2:52) in

    - "wisdom" (the development of his mind, life experience, and sound judgment)
    - "and stature" (physical growth and maturity)
    - "and in favor with God" (his spiritual growth and maturity)
    - "and [in favor with] men" (his social growth and maturity).

- Jesus was baptized in obedience, pleasing his Father (Luke 3:21-22).

- Jesus spent time alone talking with his Father, practicing the disciplines of solitude, fasting, and prayer (Luke 4:1-13, 42).
- Jesus knew Scripture and resisted temptation by quoting Scripture (Luke 4:1-32).
- Jesus let the Holy Spirit prepare him for a life of ministry and had a clear sense of what he was sent to do and what he was to accomplish (Luke 4:1, 14, 18, 42-44).

Communicating the Good News

Second, by the time Jesus began his public ministry, he was able to clearly and effectively communicate the good news of God's Kingdom to anyone and everyone who would listen. This should become your mission too. If you're going to keep growing in your faith, you need to start sharing your faith.

As you boldly explain the gospel to people and answer their deepest questions, you will find yourself exhilarated by the fact that the Holy Spirit is using you to draw lost people to the Father. As you find yourself unsure how to answer certain questions and intimidated by spiritual warfare, you will also find yourself praying more fervently, studying the Word more carefully, desiring fellowship more passionately, and experiencing God more richly. If you've ever been used by God to communicate his love to those who have never understood or even heard, you know how invigorating and spiritually fulfilling it is. If you haven't, find someone to help you get started so you won't miss this crucial part of God's great adventure.

These are big, exciting, important steps in the life of any believer. If you're making progress in these areas, congratulations. God is pleased with your heart of faith. But let us also add a word of caution. The danger here is that if you stop after just these first two steps of faith—where far too many believers stop—you'll miss the next and even more exciting part of God's plan. Indeed, you may very well stagnate in your faith and begin to lose your first true love for the Lord. For there is another essential step that Jesus modeled for those who call on his name, and if we are truly his followers, we must follow his lead.

Asking for Disciples

Third, Jesus asked his Father to show him specific men in whose lives he should invest more deeply (Luke 6:12-16). He prayed for specific men he could train into disciple makers.

This is the road less traveled by so many believers. Yet this is the real test of your spiritual growth and maturity: Are you willing and able to reproduce your faith in the life of another? For it is here, in the context of biblical discipleship, that one finds the deepest wellsprings of joy and satisfaction in the Christian faith. For it is in truly fulfilling the Great Commission that we will please the heart of God.

The Keys to Discipleship

Let's take a brief overview of the discipleship model Jesus gave us. Then we'll begin to see how to apply his key principles to our own ministry of discipleship.

Consider the following passage, which describes the moment when Jesus identified his twelve primary disciples:

> He went up on the mountain and summoned
> those whom He Himself wanted, and they came

to Him. And He appointed twelve, so that they
would be with Him and that He could send them
out to preach, and to have authority to cast out
the demons. And He appointed the twelve: Simon
(to whom He gave the name Peter), and James,
the son of Zebedee, and John the brother of James
(to them He gave the name Boanerges, which means,
"Sons of Thunder"); and Andrew, and Philip, and
Bartholomew, and Matthew, and Thomas, and James
the son of Alphaeus, and Thaddaeus, and Simon the
Zealot; and Judas Iscariot, who betrayed Him.

MARK 3:13-19

The Importance of Numbers

Scripture teaches us that Jesus did not invest in just one person. He called individuals to follow him. Then he formed a
group and built a team.

This is a key point.

One of the keys to successful investing is diversification.
If you invest all your retirement savings in one company's
stock, what if that stock's value crashes and burns? You would
be left with nothing, right? It's much wiser to invest in a
variety of stocks and bonds, from a wide range of different
types of companies in different sectors of the economy, so
that you benefit from the increased value of all such stocks
while being protected from losing everything if one stock or
one sector does poorly.

The same principle of diversification applies to spiritual
investing. What if for three years Jesus had discipled only
Judas? Despite his best efforts, Jesus would have wound up

with no one to carry on his legacy and his message when he returned to the Father.

Jesus didn't invest in just one man. He invested in a group of men from a wide range of backgrounds, including fishermen, a tax collector, and a Zealot (a political revolutionary). Each grew at a different pace. Each had a different learning style. Each learned much from the others as well as from Jesus himself. After three years, eleven of the men were ready to be apostles and carry on the work of the Kingdom. One man was a traitor. But did that traitor sink Jesus' long-term success? Not at all. Because Jesus chose a variety of men to be his disciples—in other words, because he diversified his discipleship portfolio—the failure of one didn't jeopardize his overall strategy.

Again, Jesus taught the masses, but he invested heavily in a team of twelve. He worked with a relatively small and manageable group—not twenty or fifty or one hundred. This allowed for healthy group interaction and participation. It allowed each person to have time to see Jesus up close, observe his life more carefully, and hear him talk about things he didn't discuss—or discuss in as much depth—with the masses. It gave Jesus the opportunity to know each disciple deeply and intimately enough that he could encourage each one's individual gifts and strengths and could correct each one's individual blind spots and weaknesses.

The Importance of Being Personal

The Lord's discipleship strategy began with being personal. Jesus wanted his disciples to be "with him," and this is critical. A personal relationship is essential to biblical discipleship. Indeed, as the *Revell Bible Dictionary* notes, Jesus' disciples

- lived with Jesus;
- traveled with Jesus;
- watched all Jesus did;
- listened to all Jesus said; and
- asked Jesus questions about what they observed.

This last point is important. Because Jesus' disciples knew him personally and spent lots of time with him, they felt comfortable asking a boatload of questions. They also heard other people come up and ask Jesus hard and difficult questions—and they saw him answer with grace and poise and confidence that came from knowing the Word and will of God (especially since he was the Word become flesh).

If we are going to heed Jesus' directive to go and "make disciples," we must be prepared to live up close and personal with those we seek to minister to. We must be prepared to let them travel with us and watch the way we live and listen to what we say and ask us questions. Lots of questions. Tough questions. Questions that will require us to know the Scriptures and teach the Word of Truth, not bluff our way through or offer half-baked guesses or our own philosophy and theories. Moreover, we need to know our disciples— their past histories and their present lives and their future potential.

It's important to note, of course, that discipleship comes in different phases and levels of intensity. All the apostles eventually chose to follow the Lord Jesus full-time. Thus, they were free to spend time each and every day as Jesus taught them, trained them, and traveled extensively with them. This is the best-case scenario, particularly for church leaders and leaders-in-training. But not every discipler is able to devote as much time to his disciples as Jesus did, nor is every disciple able to devote as much time to his discipler. The key is for you to spend as much time as possible with those in whom you're investing.

The Importance of Preaching

The third key point we learn about the Lord's discipleship strategy is that he taught his disciples how to preach the gospel.

Jesus not only loved his men and invested in them, but he gave them a mission and equipped them in such a way that he could "send them out to preach" the good news about the Kingdom of Heaven.

Teaching people to share their faith is central to discipleship, and that means helping someone actually develop a faith genuine enough and passionate enough to be worth sharing. It also means teaching them how to share the truth in love and gentleness and respect so as to be heard and considered and received by those who are lost.

But teaching them *how* to share their faith is not enough. We must send our disciples out to get some real-life experience. Yes, it can be difficult. Yes, it can be uncomfortable. Yes, it can even be scary to explain the message of Jesus Christ to someone who either has never heard it or has never cared to listen. But that's what the disciple's life is about: reaching the world for Christ.

We're certainly in favor of Christian service projects that teach disciples how to care for those in need, whether it's raking leaves for the elderly or hosting an international student for Thanksgiving dinner or taking a short mission trip to a foreign country to help fix or build a church building or a school. These are good and important things, and we encourage those we disciple to be engaged in them.

But we do people no favors if we shelter them from the challenge of actively sharing their faith in Jesus Christ with those who are lost and dying. Why be a disciple of Christ if not to know him and make him known? Jesus has not given us the option of simply knowing him and saying nothing. It is in the hard assignments the Master gives us that we discover the content of our character, the true measure of our devotion as disciples.

In John 14:15, Jesus said, "If you love Me, you will keep My commandments."

The apostle Peter wrote, "'Do not be frightened.' But in your hearts revere Christ as Lord. Always be prepared to give an answer to everyone who asks you to give the reason for the hope that you have" (1 Peter 3:14-15, NIV).

Sharing your faith need not be anxiety producing; it's also exhilarating. It is one of the ways we truly experience God, as his Spirit empowers us to communicate eternal truths to eternal souls.

Are you sharing your faith? Be sure to model the ministry. Lead the way. Show your disciples how it's done. Then send them out to do the same.

This was Jesus' example, and it works.[4]

---

[4]There are many wonderful resources to help you share your faith and train disciples to share theirs. *Out of the Saltshaker and into the World* by Rebecca Manley Pippert (InterVarsity Press, 1979, 1999) is a classic and helpful book. So is *The Master Plan of Evangelism* by Robert Coleman of the Billy Graham School of Evangelism (Revell, 1963, 1964, 1993). The late Bill Bright of Campus Crusade for Christ wrote a number of excellent evangelism tools, including *Witnessing without Fear* (Thomas Nelson, 1993).

The Importance of God's Power

Finally, we learn that the Lord's discipleship strategy included teaching his disciples to understand and employ the very power of God. Specifically, we learn that making disciples is about helping people to understand their place in God's Kingdom and to know that they "have authority" in the spiritual realm to win spiritual battles.

With real authority comes great power. Such power comes from being a child of the Most High God. It must be exercised wisely, and this begins with understanding our place in the universe. As Paul reminded Timothy and the church he pastored in the city of Ephesus, "Our struggle is not against flesh and blood, but against the rulers, against the powers, against the world forces of this darkness, against the spiritual forces of wickedness in the heavenly places." Then he quickly added, "Therefore, take up the full armor of God, so that you will be able to resist in the evil day, and having done everything, to stand firm" (Ephesians 6:12-13).[5]

What can we learn from this?

- We must teach people what the "full armor of God" is and how and why to put it on (Ephesians 6:10-20).
- We must teach people to stand firm against spiritual attacks and give the enemy no opening, foothold, or advantage by clothing themselves with "truth" and "righteousness" (Ephesians 6:14).
- We must teach people to be fully prepared to move quickly to communicate the Good News to every nation

---

[5] A classic book on spiritual warfare is *The Screwtape Letters* by C. S. Lewis (1942, 1996).

on the face of the earth, "having shod your feet with the preparation of the gospel of peace" (Ephesians 6:15).

- We must teach people to shield and protect themselves when the full attacks of the enemy come—to hunker in the bunker when necessary—"taking up the shield of faith with which you will be able to extinguish all the flaming arrows of the evil one" (Ephesians 6:16).
- We must teach people to go on the offensive by learning to effectively handle "the sword of the Spirit, which is the word of God" (Ephesians 6:17).
- We must teach people to "pray at all times" for all the saints and to pray that those on the front lines of the faith will "make known with boldness the mystery of the gospel" (Ephesians 6:18-19).
- We must also teach people to operate as a team, in fellowship with a tight-knit biblical community who will help them find spiritual peace rather than become spiritual casualties (Ephesians 6:21-24).

Bottom line: we must teach disciples not to trust in their own strength and power but to be constantly filled to over-flowing with the power of the Holy Spirit.[6]

We must teach them the greatness of our great God and teach them to wholly lean on the Lord Jesus, who reminded us in the Great Commission that he has been given "all authority in heaven and on earth" and *"therefore"* we can go and make disciples of all nations. And we can rest on his

[6]A good book to read on the role of the Holy Spirit in our lives and the power he provides us to develop Christlike character and guard against sin is *The Holy Spirit: Activating God's Power in Your Life* by Billy Graham (Thomas Nelson, 1978, 1988).

promise that he will be with us always, "to the very end of the age" (Matthew 28:18-20, NIV).

QUESTIONS

1. What are the three most dramatic ways Jesus has changed your life since you've become a Christian? How might this testimony help younger believers grow?

2. Read Mark 3:13-15. What are four distinctive elements of the way Jesus discipled men? How would you say you're doing in each of these four areas?

3. Look up the following passages. Describe the role of the Holy Spirit in the life of Jesus and his disciples.
   • Matthew 12:18
   • Mark 1:10
   • Luke 4:1, 14, 18
   • John 16:7-15

4. Look up the following passages. Describe the role the Holy Spirit should play in our lives as disciples and disciple makers.
   • John 4:24
   • Galatians 5:16
   • Ephesians 5:18
   • Ephesians 6:17

5. Evaluate yourself. Do you ask God every morning to fill you with his Holy Spirit? Do you continue to ask him throughout the day to keep you filled with his Spirit? How well would you say you understand what it means to do ministry in the power of the Holy Spirit? In what areas would you like to improve?

TESTIMONY: SYRACUSE
DR. T. E. KOSHY

One day, Brother Bakht Singh gave me a verse God was showing him for me, Isaiah 43:19: "Behold, I will do something new, now it will spring forth; will you not be aware of it? I will even make a roadway in the wilderness, rivers in the desert."

As I studied that verse and meditated on it, I found myself drawn to Isaiah 43:1-3 as well. "Do not fear, for I have redeemed you; I have called you by name; you are Mine! When you pass through the waters, I will be with you; and through the rivers, they will not overflow you. When you walk through the fire, you will not be scorched, nor will the flame burn you. For I am the LORD your God, the Holy One of Israel, your Savior."

Many of my friends believed it was time for me to return

to India from England to assist Brother Bakht Singh in the ministry there. But Bakht Singh believed that the Lord was preparing me for a new ministry in the United States. Neither of us knew what lay ahead. But I appreciated his confidence and his encouragement. So in the fall of 1965, I left England and arrived in America as a graduate student at the S. I. Newhouse School of Public Communications at Syracuse University. It was several hours northwest of New York City, but light-years from anything I had ever previously experienced.

The mid-1960s was the height of the countercultural revolution on American college campuses. President John F. Kennedy had been assassinated in 1963. The Vietnam War was escalating. The antiwar protests were escalating. The Beatles and the Grateful Dead were the rage. The drug culture was exploding. Young people were experimenting with new ideas, new politics, and new drugs, spurred on by LSD gurus such as Timothy Leary. Then came the race riots and, in 1968, the assassinations of Robert Kennedy and Martin Luther King Jr. You name it, young people were doing it. Whatever veneer there was of America abiding by biblical values was being blown to pieces. American college campuses were in real turmoil, and international students were caught in the cross fire.

As a Christian coming from India and England to S.U.—which, like many major American universities, was founded by believers in Jesus Christ (in this case, devout Methodists)—seeing such cultural chaos and outright rejection of God really shocked and saddened me. No sooner did I arrive than I began to think I must have made a terrible mistake in coming after all. I was alone, without friends and without fellowship. One day I found myself on my knees, crying and praying and saying, "Lord, why did I come to this country?"

The Lord ministered to me and gently said, "Koshy, I have brought you here for a purpose."

"But, Lord, I am going through all kinds of shocks. Culture shock. Weather shock. Identity shock. Homesickness. Loneliness."

Then the Lord spoke very directly to me. "Koshy, you are a Christian, and you see how miserable you feel here in this 'Christian' country. But have you stopped to think of the needs of others, particularly international students?"

"Lord," I replied, "let the Americans take care of them. I am a stranger in the midst of strangers. These people are Hindus and Muslims and Communists and atheists. They don't care for you. Why should I care for them?"

Then the Lord said to me, "But, Koshy, I care for them. Not only that, I loved them enough to die for them."

"But, Lord, it is hard to convert them," I said, still believing that the task of ministry was to look at unbelievers as targets for conversion.

But the Lord said to me, "Koshy, I don't want you to convert a single soul. Don't look at them as targets for conversion. Don't do anything just to convert them. I am the God who loves. I am the God who cares. But I have no hands to touch them. I have no feet to go to them. They are lonely. They are looking for a friend to turn to. Won't you be my hands to minister to them? Won't you be my feet to go to them? You do the loving. You do the caring. You do the serving, and I will do the converting."

"All right, Lord," I said, "but how do I go about it? What do I do?"

"The way to the heart of people is through their stomachs. These students are lonely. They are looking for friends and a good meal. You invite them."

"But, Lord, there are so many of them. I don't know how to cook. I don't have any recipes. I don't know how to make meals for people from so many different countries."

Then the Lord said to me, "Don't worry; I will help you."

I remembered the Scriptures from Isaiah with which Brother Bakht Singh had encouraged me. Suddenly it felt like the very Word of God became alive. It became flesh. Even though I myself did not love all these foreign students, I became willing to do what God wanted me to do.

When I made that commitment, my heart was filled with love for the students around me. I began to pray with new zeal for the power to tell others on campus about Jesus, the one who loves *all* the people of the world. I felt as though the Lord walked into that room—that lonely room where I was kneeling down—and picked me up in his arms and gave me a good bear hug.

"Koshy," he said, "just because you are mine does not mean you won't have trials. It is not when you go through affluence but through afflictions that you realize how precious I am to you. So I am allowing you to go through these trials and problems to mold you, to shape you, so that you may know who I am."

Overwhelmed by his gentleness and tender loving mercies, right there on my knees I said to the Lord, "All right. I am willing to do it."

So, trusting entirely in the Lord, I began inviting students to my tiny bachelor's apartment and began cooking meals for them and befriending them. I was chief cook and dishwasher.

In fact, I told the Lord that I would buy the groceries, bring them to my room, and then at the stove I would kneel down and say, "Lord, you said you will do it. This is your opportunity to do the cooking. I will start shaking the salt. When you think enough has gone in, you can stop me."

And you know what? The Lord honored that prayer.

Students would come and eat the food, and they would say, "Oh, it is so delicious. Who did the cooking? Could you give us the recipe?"

"I don't have any recipe," I told them. How was I supposed to tell a bunch of agnostics and atheists that God was helping me do the cooking?

But some of them were offended because they didn't know how to cook and here I was making good food and they wanted to learn how to do it. So some would say, "Koshy, I thought you were our friend; that is why you invited us. If you don't care to give the recipe, I don't care for your food."

Then I would whisper and say, "If you insist, God helped me."

They would look at me and say, "I thought something was wrong with you. Now I know for sure—you're crazy." Some of them wouldn't even come back. Even if I saw them on campus, they wouldn't look at me. That was hard for me because it seemed like such a trivial thing.

But you know what was extraordinary? Many came back again and again. Some would say to me, "I never believed in a personal God. But the moment I walked in, I felt something here. There is peace. There is joy. Tell me more about your experiences. I want to know this God of yours." And I would tell them. Some of them would say they wanted to know more. So I would give them copies of the New Testament. I started a Bible study.

Then God brought to Syracuse a wonderful Indian woman, Indira Perry, a strong believer who knew Brother Bakht Singh very well. She was a great medical doctor, a brilliant eye surgeon. She had a great love for students and evangelism and discipleship—and she knew how to cook. By God's grace, we were married on October 14, 1967, at North Syracuse Baptist Church, moved out of my tiny apartment into a more spacious home, and began serving the Lord and these students.

In 1969, Brother Bakht Singh visited us in Syracuse and was encouraged to see what God was doing in the lives of students and nonstudents through our ministry. In 1970, he visited again and told us that as evangelists, our responsibility was not only to see men and women coming to know the Lord, but also to disciple them through the Christ-centered local church. After all, in the New Testament we see that the Lord Jesus Christ is the head of the church and does everything through the church, including training and equipping disciples to do his Father's will (see Ephesians 4:11-16 and 1 Corinthians 12).

On Brother Bakht Singh's advice, therefore, we changed the weekly Bible study we were leading in our home to what we called the International Assembly, a biblical church based on Acts 2:42, with a vision to make disciples of all nations. Prayerfully, we launched a Sunday morning worship service,

Sunday school classes, and midweek Bible classes. Then we moved our weekly friendship lunch to Sundays, right after church.

We couldn't believe what happened. In a given month, we would have about five hundred students coming to our home. It was all so exciting, hosting parties together with the living God and having the joy of seeing Hindus, Muslims, Buddhists, atheists, and people from all over the world tasting the love of God in a practical way. Many received Christ as their Savior and Lord. Many were discipled, encouraged, and equipped in their faith through the activities of the church. And many went back to their countries with the desire to plant similar local churches in their own communities, since the principles of the New Testament church are transferable to any country, any culture, at any time.

This, in turn, led to my becoming the evangelical chaplain at S.U. in 1972, which despite occasional—and sometimes intense—resistance from various faculty members, and even from the administration itself over the years, began to give me a wonderfully strategic position of credibility to influence the entire campus and community.

As the Lord directed us, we launched a free annual Thanksgiving dinner for internationals. We started a free weekly friendship luncheon for internationals and Americans on Thursdays. To this day, these lunches often draw between one hundred fifty and two hundred students each week, all of whom are looking for a little food, a little kindness, and someone to listen to them.

In 1972, the Lord also led us to launch International Friendship Evangelism, a nonprofit ministry to help other churches learn to build bridges of relationships cross-culturally and catch a vision for a hospitality-based ministry to the some half-million foreign students in the United States—many of them from countries hostile or closed to the gospel—plus thousands more businessmen and diplomats.

Along the way, we have prayed fervently for God to send us volunteers and interns and staff we could disciple and involve in the ministry, and the Lord has always graciously and generously provided. Which is wonderful because we could never accomplish on our own what the Lord has called us to do. Nor would we want to.

Because we have trained others to do what God has taught us to do, others have caught the vision and begun similar ministries all over the world. We do not have a large ministry or building or budget. But by God's grace, he is using us to touch the lives of men and women all over the world with the love of Jesus Christ and in turn make disciples of all nations.

Brother Bakht Singh was right. The Lord who knew my heart was beginning a new thing. He had brought me to a place where I could reach not only the influential people of India but also influential people from every nation on the face of the earth by reaching out to them to make friends, not converts, and by showing them love and hospitality and serving them a warm, home-cooked meal. It was definitely not my way. It was completely God's way. But it was the right way, and for several decades now, it has borne remarkable fruit.

CHAPTER FIVE
PRAYERFULLY CHOOSE

I have brought you glory on earth by finishing the work you gave me to do. . . . I have revealed you to those whom you gave me out of the world. They were yours; you gave them to me and they have obeyed your word.

JESUS CHRIST (JOHN 17:4, 6, NIV)

Are you ready to start investing, even if a bit anxious?

Great. Here are some practical suggestions to help you get started.

The first question you'll face is, whom should I invest in? Consider the following verses:

It was at this time that He went off to the mountain to pray, and He spent the whole night in prayer to God. And when day came, He called His disciples to Him and chose twelve of them.

LUKE 6:12-13

> You did not choose Me but I chose you, and
> appointed you that you would go and bear fruit, and
> that your fruit would remain, so that whatever you
> ask of the Father in My name He may give to you.
>
> JOHN 15:16

Look closely. Who chose whom? Did the disciples choose Jesus, or did Jesus choose them? How did Jesus know whom to choose? Who were these people? Were they complete strangers to Jesus? What lessons can we draw from these Scriptures?

As God raises up a new global movement of disciple makers, he wants us to understand a foundational principle: we don't choose whom to disciple. God chooses for us. This is good news, especially for those who have never discipled anyone before. The burden and pressure isn't on you to find an open, hungry heart. The burden is on you to pray. The Lord will bring someone to you—and the right someone at that.

Ignore this principle at your peril. Why? Because while discipleship is clearly God's work, we must always be careful to do God's work in God's way. Having discovered how important discipleship is to God's plan and purpose for our lives, we must not now suddenly yank the steering wheel out of God's hands and begin driving our own way.

Remember what the Lord said to Samuel in 1 Samuel 16:7. "Do not look at his appearance or at the height of his stature, because I have rejected him; for God sees not as man sees, for man looks at the outward appearance, but the LORD looks at the heart."

Only God knows what truly lies within a man's heart.

Only God knows the true potential of a man. We cannot really know on our own. Not for sure. That's why the process of choosing disciples must really be a process of prayer, even fasting, as we seek to know the specific people in whose lives God wants us to invest.

God may show you some specific person or group of people right away. But it also may take some time. Our advice: don't rush the process of trying to find someone. Don't select someone simply because he's eager or because he is highly recommended or because there doesn't seem to be anyone else. Don't select someone just because you're eager or because this person strikes you as the "perfect" disciple. That may or may not be. The key is to get on your knees in prayer and stay there asking God to be clear with you. Don't let up until he answers. Maybe this will take a few days or a few weeks or a few months. Maybe the person who seems so "perfect" as you begin to pray turns out not to be so "perfect" after some time in prayer and some time watching his life.

It is very tempting to do what the prophet Samuel did and look at the outward appearance. But instead we must follow Solomon's admonition in Proverbs 3:5-6 to trust in the Lord with all our heart and lean not on our own understanding. This is critically important in beginning a discipleship relationship. In all your ways acknowledge the Lord, and he will make your paths straight.

Don't make a decision too quickly. Don't get ahead of God. Trust him. Wait on him. He knows your heart, and he is excited about your desire to disciple someone. He will bring along the right person at the right time as you love him and serve him faithfully and patiently and prayerfully.

Fishing in Your Own Pond

As we begin to pray for people to invest in, it's important to observe an interesting fact about the men the Father chose for Jesus to disciple: *Jesus was familiar with them.* Not just because he was omniscient. Jesus knew them because they were not strangers. They were compatriots. They had been following him for some time, hearing him preach and teach and watching him up close. They had been able to observe him, and he had been able to observe them over a period of time. Thus, he had the opportunity to get a sense of their character and capabilities (and lack thereof).

This is an important model. It is very likely that God will choose individuals you should disciple from people you're already ministering to or at least people within your general "orbit." Sure, God can bring people out of nowhere whom he wants you to disciple. That's certainly happened to us. But often he fishes men out of the ministry pond in which you're already working.

Therefore, you need to follow Jesus' example and be actively engaged in a ministry where you're serving a group of people. If you're a pastor or ministry staff member or active lay leader, you are probably already ministering to a larger pool of people than the average layperson. If you're just getting interested in ministry, perhaps it's time for you to start teaching a small-group Bible study. Or teaching a Sunday school class. Or serving in the music ministry. Or leading or working on a ministry team that cares for the poor or the disabled or that helps people develop vocational skills or discover their spiritual gifts.

The key is that you need to begin by being in the precise

ministry to which God has called you, one that puts you in contact with groups of people and specifically in contact with potential leaders.

As you minister to this group, scan the horizon for people in whom God *might* want you to invest.

Let's say you and your wife lead a home fellowship group in your church. Is God pointing out to you a young couple who seem to be particularly hungry to know God, seem to show real spiritual promise, and might be able to minister to others someday, perhaps even in full-time vocational Christian work?

Or let's say you teach a Sunday school class of high school kids. Is God pointing out to you a few young people who really seem hungry to know more and could be trained to be youth leaders who will share their faith with unbelievers and encourage the faith of younger believers?

Or maybe you're in the church's choir or lead a group of musicians or serve as an usher or work in the church office as an administrative assistant.

Look around you. Whom do you see who is younger in the faith than you, hungry to learn more, and might really appreciate getting some special attention from you and even being taken under your wing on a spiritual adventure? Keep your eye on promising believers, but again, remember not to judge by outward appearances. Let God give you guidance and discernment. Ask him to direct you and clarify his perfect will for you.

Also, keep in mind that discipleship is not a program—it's a way of life. Therefore, we wouldn't recommend that you set up "discipleship classes" to "disciple" large groups of people at once. Or create a "discipleship month" campaign in your church to "recruit" new disciples. Or send around a clipboard to let people sign up to be discipled if they are so interested. There's no biblical model for such an approach.

Remember: Evangelism is the place to cast a wide net. Discipleship is the place to be selective and personal.

It would be great to be able to disciple everybody the minute you and your church get the vision for spiritual investing. But rarely is that practically possible, since there usually aren't enough trained disciple makers in most churches at the beginning. The key is getting started by taking one step at a time. That means focusing on finding a few specific individuals—"faithful men who will be able to teach others also"—not appealing to large groups.

Look in your own pond for people with potential. Look for people who are drawn to what you're interested in and who seem to be going where you're going. Look for people who would allow you to be engaged in discipleship while never missing a beat in the area of ministry to which God has already called you. In fact, look for people who perhaps could eventually lead the very ministry you're currently leading—people who could be your successors.

Discipleship is not supposed to be a separate function from the ministry in which you're already engaged. It should be central to what you're already doing. It should be a natural extension of the ministry you already have—just more personally and intensely focused on reliable people who will eventually be qualified to teach others as well.

Most important, keep on praying. God will prepare the hearts of the right people for you to disciple and make these people crystal clear to you.

A note here to parents: Scripture teaches that the most

important disciplers for children are their parents. Consider Deuteronomy 6:1-12; Proverbs 22:6; and 1 Thessalonians 2, particularly verses 7-12. These are just a few of the biblical admonitions to parents to teach their children the Scriptures, raise up their children in the way that they uniquely should go, and care for children as gentle, tender mothers and as encouraging, exhorting, challenging fathers.

However, while children are a parent's *top* priority, it is important to note that they are not a parent's *sole* priority.

In the Great Commission, Jesus did not say, "Go and make disciples of all nations—*unless you have children and are therefore too busy, too tired, and too distracted by all the necessities of parenthood.*" Nor did he say, "Go and make disciples of all nations—*unless you have children and have decided that your mission field is your children and they must be the sole focus of your teaching and spiritual encouragement.*"

What did Jesus say? He told us to go and make disciples *"of all nations."*

Leading our children to Christ and helping them grow and mature in their faith is our God-given charge and an enormous responsibility. That responsibility includes modeling for our children the importance of reaching out to people outside our own family, outside our own culture, and outside our own nation, to help them find Christ.

Looking for F.A.T. Christians

God is looking for F.A.T. people.

It may sound silly, but it's true.

He is looking for men and women who are *faithful, available,* and *teachable.*

As you consider specific people to disciple and wait on the Lord for guidance, here are some character traits to look for and ask God about:

Faithful

In the parable of the talents, we learn that the disciple who truly pleases God is a "good and faithful servant," of whom the Lord Jesus can say, "You have been faithful with a few things; I will put you in charge of many things" (Matthew 25:21, 23, NIV). Moreover, we learn in the same parable that what displeases and angers God is people who are "lazy" and refuse to take action or risks for him (Matthew 25:26).

God is looking for true disciples who have

- the *humility* to do small projects first rather than be so proud and arrogant that they demand to be given "big" and "important" projects right from the beginning; and
- the *trustworthiness* to do small projects with such excellence—such thoroughness and completeness— that they earn the opportunity to be given more responsibility.

What does this mean in the context of discipleship?

Let's say that you are led to invest in someone in particular. You start praying for guidance. As you do, start looking at his life more closely. Does he show signs of faithfulness in small but significant areas of life?

- If this person is in your small-group Bible study or Sunday school class, does he attend consistently and show up on time, or is he constantly absent, late, and offering excuses?

- If you give him a small task to complete—bringing food for a fellowship dinner or researching all the New Testament references to baptism for an upcoming Bible study or scouting out places to hold a retreat weekend—can he be trusted to complete the task thoroughly, eagerly, and with enthusiasm rather than complaints?
- If he hits a roadblock while trying to complete a task, does he show some creative problem-solving abilities to get the job done anyway, or is he immediately immobilized?
- Is he a "go the extra mile" kind of Christian, willing to give more to a project than was asked of him, or does he cut corners and try to do as little as possible to get by?
- Does he RSVP to invitations, return phone calls and reply to e-mails as promptly as possible, and respond to various requests for help around the church without even being asked personally, or does he seem disinterested in good manners and disrespectful of the time and feelings of others?

The key to identifying a person's faithfulness is observing his response to requests and assignments.

If he is asked to do something small or large, what is his modus operandi? Does he act quickly and cheerfully and completely or not?

These are just a few ways to observe and measure basic faithfulness. But hopefully they will give you a glimpse of what you should be looking for and certainly what God is looking for.

That said, be careful not to confuse *faithfulness* with *faith*—trust in the greatness of our great God—in a young believer. The whole point of discipleship is to help someone's faith grow and increase and mature so the believer is able to do larger and tougher and riskier tasks for God as the months and years go by. It is unlikely that the person you will invest in will have deep reservoirs of refined and tested and active faith . . . yet. So don't look for him to have that which the Holy Spirit of God will use you to help build.

No, what you're looking for is basic *faithfulness*, loyalty and trustworthiness and conscientiousness, accuracy and attention to detail, and attention to the needs and concerns of others. These are some essential building blocks of a disciple of Jesus Christ.

Available

A person's faithfulness is measured by his spiritual loyalty and commitment to the things of the Lord. A person's *availability* is measured by his internal motivation to serve the Lord.

At the most basic level, of course, a person must literally be available and internally motivated to carve time out of his schedule to meet with you. It makes no sense—and does no good—to force or prod or even coax a person to be discipled. If a person doesn't want what you have to offer—if he can't or won't make himself literally, physically, consistently, even somewhat sacrificially available—then he may simply not yet be ready to be discipled, or you may not be the one God has chosen to work with him or vice versa.

112

It is in the arena of evangelism that we persistently pursue those who don't want to hear. In the arena of discipleship, we want to focus only on those Paul described as "faithful men who will be able to teach others also" (2 Timothy 2:2). If a person isn't internally motivated to be discipled, he won't be faithful or reliable to teach others. He isn't ready. So don't force the issue.

But being "available" is more than a matter of time and schedule. It is also a matter of the heart. It is about whether or not a person has a deep hunger after God. After all, God is more interested in our *being* than our *doing*. What God is looking for in a person—and what you should be looking for as well—is a readiness, a willingness, indeed an eagerness to be used by God to advance his Kingdom. God is looking not just for the availability of a person's calendar but the availability of a person's heart. He's looking for someone who is motivated from deep within to learn more, grow more, do more, and accomplish more for God than he has in the past.

In Isaiah 6:8, the prophet described his own response to God's call. "I heard the voice of the Lord, saying, 'Whom shall I send, and who will go for Us?' Then I said, 'Here am I. Send me!'"

Clearly, Isaiah was available. He had the kind of heart God is looking for in those who would be his true disciples, a heart that says, "Here am I. Send me!"

How, then, might you spot signs of availability? Here are some suggestions:

- Is this person active or passive? Does he take the initiative to serve God and make his name known— or at least show a desire to do so—or would he be more accurately classified as a "spiritual couch potato," more interested in sitting and listening to leaders talk about faith and risk and reaching the world for Christ than getting up and actually exercising his spiritual muscles?

- Does he voraciously read books or other materials that give him a clearer, fuller picture of the Christian life, evangelism, missions, and leadership?

- Does he seek out sermons and conferences and retreats that will help him grow and mature in his faith?

- Does he pray for opportunities to help his family, friends, and colleagues come to know Christ and grow in their faith?

- Does he show interest in going with you to practice sharing his faith?

- Does he show interest in going on a short-term mission project to tell others about the Lord?

- Does he show any interest in full-time vocational Christian ministry, even if he's not sure if that's precisely what God wants him to do?

- Does he show willingness to give financially to those in need, and does he contribute generously from his income to the church and to missionaries and various Christian ministries?

- Does he initiate personal relationships within the body of Christ, develop strong, close friendships, and seek out the advice, accountability, and encouragement of others, while also offering the same?

- Does he make regular time in his schedule for reading the Word and communicating with the Lord through prayer?

Again, these are just a few ways to begin to gauge a person's availability to know the Lord and serve him with courage and boldness, but hopefully they will be helpful in your process of evaluation and prayer.

Teachable

Being faithful is a measure of how one responds to requests and assignments. Being available is a measure of how internally motivated one is to serve God and take the initiative to be used by him. What, then, does it mean to be *teachable*?

It is essential that you truly understand what teachability means, for it is arguably the most important characteristic of all in the context of discipleship. Whether a person is teachable or not will determine whether you have any chance of being helpful and effective in helping him grow and mature in his faith to the point of being able to spiritually reproduce in the lives of others.

Let's be clear: being teachable means having the *willingness* to learn *and* to put into practice what you have learned.

In other words, a person is not teachable simply because he attends your small-group Bible study every week. That's being faithful, not teachable. A person is not teachable because he does his Bible study homework or has daily quiet times or memorizes Scripture or goes to church every week or goes to Bible college or attends seminary. These may be signs of availability, but they are not necessarily signs of teachability.

The true test of someone's teachability is whether he puts into practice what he is learning from the Lord through you or others.

The apostle James put it this way:

Prove yourselves doers of the word, and not merely
hearers who delude themselves. For if anyone is a hearer
of the word and not a doer, he is like a man who looks
at his natural face in a mirror; for once he has looked at
himself and gone away, he has immediately forgotten
what kind of person he was. But one who looks
intently at the perfect law, the law of liberty, and abides
by it, not having become a forgetful hearer but an
effectual doer, this man will be blessed in what he does.

JAMES 1:22-25

Here are some ways that you might identify someone who
is teachable:

- If you explain the scriptural importance of being
  baptized, does this person show an eagerness to be
  baptized at the earliest possible opportunity (if he has
  not already been baptized since truly giving his life to
  Jesus Christ and becoming born again)? Or does he
  either chafe and resist being baptized or show little
  or no interest or even procrastinate and delay?
- If you explain the Bible's emphasis on developing a
  disciplined prayer life—and model this in your own
  personal life and how you lead your Bible study or
  Sunday school class or other form of ministry group—
  does he begin to pray more regularly and faithfully
  and systematically, or does he show little progress in
  the area of prayer?

- If you make the biblical case to be careful not to swear or tell coarse or improper jokes or constantly criticize others or be routinely sarcastic and cutting in remarks to others, does this person take this admonition to heart and begin to change, or does he disregard what he has been taught?
- If you explain what the Scriptures teach about the need to control one's temper and be quick to listen and slow to anger, does this person begin asking God to help him rein in his emotions and keep his cool, or does he seem unwilling to put into practice what he's been taught?
- Bottom line: does this person seem willing to practice what's been preached?

All of us have a learning curve, of course. All of us have sins that so easily entangle us. All of us have a difficult time changing, much less changing quickly. So again, you're not looking to see if a person is perfect. Rest assured, he won't be.

The question concerns whether he responds positively to solid, wise, and loving biblical instruction and counsel and begins to demonstrate real life change as a result, or whether he seems cool, even callous, to putting into practice what God is teaching him through the Word.

A word of encouragement: as you begin to minister to others and engage in a life of discipleship, you might be surprised, even discouraged, by how few people in the world really have teachable hearts and spirits. Don't be.

First of all, remember that the road to the abundant, eternal life is very narrow indeed. That's just the way it is.

Second, and even more important, rather than being

discouraged, be determined to find "faithful men" who will be qualified not just to learn from you but "to teach others also." You're not looking for many. You're looking for a few who will benefit enormously from your investment in them. Therefore, rather than having soaring expectations built on quantity, have specific expectations built on quality.

Remember the parable of the seed and the sower we discussed earlier?

[Jesus] told them many things in parables, saying: "A farmer went out to sow his seed. As he was scattering the seed, some fell along the path, and the birds came and ate it up. Some fell on rocky places, where it did not have much soil. It sprang up quickly, because the soil was shallow. But when the sun came up, the plants were scorched, and they withered because they had no root. Other seed fell among thorns, which grew up and choked the plants. Still other seed fell on good soil, where it produced a crop—a hundred, sixty or thirty times what was sown. . . . Listen then to what the parable of the sower means: When anyone hears the message about the kingdom and does not understand it, the evil one comes and snatches away what was sown in their heart. This is the seed sown along the path. The seed falling on rocky ground refers to someone who hears the word and at once receives it with joy. But since they have no root, they last only a short time. When trouble or persecution comes because of the word, they quickly fall away. The seed falling among the thorns refers to someone who hears the word, but the worries of this life and the deceitfulness of wealth choke the word, making it unfruitful. But the seed falling on good soil refers to someone who hears the word and understands it. This is the one who produces a crop, yielding a hundred, sixty or thirty times what was sown."

MATTHEW 13:3-8, 18-23 (NIV)

Not every heart is a willing heart. Not every heart is "good soil." But we shouldn't be discouraged. The Lord is looking for a few good men in whose lives you can invest. The returns on that investment will astound you. Therefore, stay focused on quality, not quantity, and bless the many by investing in a few.

After all, a true disciple is a contagious Christian. Someone who knows the Lord and has had a person heavily invest in his life is brimming with spiritual capital. Non-Christians will be drawn to him, to ask him what is so special about his life. Then he will have the opportunity to share Christ and perhaps lead them into the Kingdom. Christians will also be drawn to him, to ask him why he seems so different from them. Again, he will have the opportunity to share the joy of discipleship with them and perhaps lead them into a deeper, closer, and dramatically more fulfilling walk with God.

So remember: F.A.T. content.

That's what God is looking for in his true disciples. We should be on the lookout for it as well, as we earnestly pray for God to show us people in whose lives he wants us to invest.

The above criteria, of course, are suggestions to help, not to be taken as dogmatic. Do we mean to imply that people who don't display these three qualities should never be discipled?

No. Everyone who gives his life to Jesus Christ and is born again needs to be taught how to live the Christian life and how to grow in his faith. In leading someone to Christ or meeting a new believer for the first time, you may have no way of knowing whether he is faithful, available, and/or teachable. Don't write off such believers based on some kind of human evaluation process. That's not what we're saying at all.

The key is to pray and trust the Lord to show you the right thing to do. We are simply encouraging you to keep in mind the scriptural principles of spiritual investment. We want to help you see that wise and careful investing produces fabulous returns.

Yes, there will be failures and casualties. Even Jesus had a Judas. But keep in mind that the people who will most likely respond favorably to your discipleship will be people who are faithful, available, and teachable.

QUESTIONS

1. Read Luke 6:12-13 and John 15:16. Who chose the Twelve—Jesus or the Father? What lessons should we draw from the process Jesus went through?

2. Read 1 Samuel 16:7. Who chose David to be king of Israel—Samuel or God? What is God looking for in the leaders he raises up for his people? What is he not looking for?

3. What principles is God trying to teach us in these passages about how to find people we are to disciple?

4. Who are some younger believers in your "fishing pond" whom God seems to be putting on your heart as potential "Timothys"? Next to each name, make notes about their F.A.T. content.

TESTIMONY: MRS. INDIRA KOSHY, MD

I grew up in the city of Ahmedabad, India.

My mother, Dinah, was a believer in Jesus Christ. But my father, John Perry, was not. One night during a revival meeting, an American missionary gave an invitation for people to give their lives to Jesus Christ. I went forward, and that is how I came to know the Lord as a born-again Christian. Though I was only eleven years old, my life turned around 180 degrees. I could almost immediately see God beginning to transform my attitudes and values and giving me a new-found passion for schoolwork and for reading.

When I was about thirteen, the choir director in the Methodist church I attended asked me if I was saved. I explained that I had gone forward to receive Christ at a revival meeting about two years earlier. But beyond that,

I didn't know what else to do. I wasn't reading the Bible, and I didn't really have anyone to encourage me. I started to cry. Very kindly and gently, the choir director, a man named Lincoln Desai, gave me four Scripture passages that would form the centerpieces of my life.

The first verse he gave me was John 1:12. "As many as received Him, to them He gave the right to become children of God, even to those who believe in His name." Mr. Desai explained that I was now a child of God, part of his very own family.

The second reference he gave me was Isaiah 53:5-6. "He was pierced through for our transgressions, He was crushed for our iniquities; the chastening for our well-being fell upon Him, and by His scourging we are healed. All of us like sheep have gone astray, each of us has turned to his own way; but the LORD has caused the iniquity of us all to fall on Him."

Mr. Desai asked me, "Where are your sins now?"

"They're on Jesus," I replied.

"Yes, that's right. Why, then, are you crying?"

He was right, and as he shared with me these Scriptures, I began to feel better.

The third verse he gave me was Revelation 3:20. "Behold, I stand at the door and knock; if anyone hears My voice and opens the door, I will come in to him and will dine with him, and he with Me." Mr. Desai explained how by opening the door of my heart, Jesus had come into my life and was eager to talk with me and love me and guide me throughout my life.

The fourth passage he gave me was Ephesians 2:8-9. "By grace you have been saved through faith; and that not of yourselves, it is the gift of God; not as a result of works, so that no one may boast." Mr. Desai taught me that I was saved by God's love, mercy, and unmerited favor and that there was nothing I could do to lose my salvation or stop being one of God's precious children.

For the first time, I now had true assurance of my salvation. A little smile broke out on my face, and my spirits began to lift. Then Mr. Desai taught me four things I needed in order to grow as a disciple of the Lord Jesus Christ. First, I needed to start reading the Bible daily, for God's Word is our spiritual food. Second, I needed to start praying all the time, for talking to the Lord is as essential as breathing. Third, I needed to be in regular fellowship with other believers, for the church is like our family, giving us comfort and encouragement. Fourth, I needed to start witnessing for the Lord and serving his people and those who didn't yet know him, because serving the Lord is our spiritual exercise. I listened carefully and started putting into practice everything Mr. Desai said, and I began to have a hunger for God like I'd never experienced before.

Mr. Desai soon noticed that I was becoming a voracious reader, so he started loaning me lots of Christian books. Every few days I would return the books I'd finished reading, and he would lend me more. As I read about men and women giving their lives to serve the Lord full-time as missionaries all over the world, I began to ask, "Lord, please give me a profession where I can meet new people and tell them how wonderful you are." I prayed much during my teenage years, and by God's grace, my grades in school just kept going up and up and up. I had so much peace, and I was really concentrating. After that, I went to a science college and then applied to Vellore Christian Medical College in southern India.

Brother Bakht Singh used to come to Ahmedabad for special meetings, teaching the Scriptures and leading prayer and worship. My father's older brother, Paul Perry, was an elder of a local church patterned after the New Testament–model churches Bakht Singh was planting all over India, and he was a good friend of Brother Singh. But my father was not.

My father didn't like Brother Bakht Singh, not at all. He didn't know him personally like my uncle did. Every time my father heard Bakht Singh's name, he got mad. He never allowed us to go see him because he thought Brother Singh and his associates were antichurch, since many people trusting Christ were then leaving the Methodist churches to attend the churches Brother Singh was planting. That made my father very angry, though, again, I don't think he was even a believer. That's just how my father was. Eventually, however, I got to see and hear Brother Bakht Singh in person when I went to Vellore for three full days of interviews to get into medical school. I was fascinated by him and blessed by the way God used him to teach the Word and challenge us young people to walk with Christ.

During those three days, my father came down from northern India to visit me. To my great surprise, upon his arrival my father actually accepted the invitation of the man in whose home he was staying to attend a meeting Brother Bakht Singh was leading. My father figured that since he was far from home and nobody he knew would be there, it would simply be polite to accept his host's invitation and

attend. What happened when he got to the Christian meeting, however, stunned everyone, especially me. No sooner
had my father arrived for the very first meeting than the Holy
Spirit moved Brother Singh to go straight toward him like an
arrow and ask him, "Who are you, and what is your name?"

My father, taken completely off guard, introduced himself.

"You are Paul Perry's brother," Brother Singh said.

"Yes, I am."

"You have not come here on your own," Brother Singh
told him. "God has brought you here."

Then Brother Bakht Singh turned to the host family who
had brought my father to the meeting and said, "Bring his
luggage here. He is not leaving this place. He is going to stay
with me."

Suddenly my father found himself staying with Brother
Singh for three days. He attended all the meetings. He got to
know Bakht Singh personally. And in the process, my father
came to know Jesus Christ as his personal Savior and Lord.
It was a complete miracle.

After three days, my father came to see me to find out
whether I had been selected for medical school or not. As
I saw him coming, I realized that I'd never noticed he was
such a handsome man. His face was shining. As he came
near, I felt like joking with him, something I had never dared
to do because he had been such a serious, angry man all my
life. But I could see, even from a distance, what a completely
transformed man he had become. Then my father took me
to Brother Bakht Singh, praising God for all the wonderful
things he was doing. What a surprise.

When we arrived, he told Brother Singh, "Brother, in my

family—in my home—my daughter Indira is the one who is most like you and your people."

Brother Singh was very happy. Immediately he knelt down and prayed for my schooling in Vellore. He said to me, "Consider this your home. Please come here anytime."

By God's grace, I was accepted into medical school and began attending the church Brother Singh had planted there. Along the way, I met many godly students and older Christian women who were great role models for me and really encouraged me and helped me grow in the Lord. They helped me discover more deeply the joys of worship and prayer and evangelism and discipleship, and we worked together very closely to reach the unsaved students and nominal Christians who were part of the school.

I remember in particular a wonderful missionary lady from Australia named Miss North who took me and several other young women under her wing. Probably around forty-five years old and single, she was a member of Brother Bakht Singh's assembly and a great encouragement to us. She was very godly and gentle. She loved to worship the Lord, and she really loved us and cared for us. She actually lived in our dorm, as did several other missionary women. Once when I got sick, she insisted that I come and stay in her room for a week, and she looked after me. My friends all had similar stories of Miss North's kindness and hospitality.

Every evening we had a time of Bible study and prayer in the dorms. About ten to twelve women would attend, and we would rotate leading the group. Miss North joined us almost every night and participated in our discussions, answering our questions and offering advice and exhortation when we needed it. Then we started all-night prayer meetings once a month, and she came to those as well. We would start around 8 p.m. and go to about 6 a.m., beseeching the Lord to do something mighty and miraculous in our midst. Praying together is a great way to get to know people, and we really enjoyed getting to know Miss North and having her care for us the way she did.

Mother Brand was another wonderful Christian missionary woman who loved me and invested in me. I don't remember when we first started calling her Mother Brand, but I do remember she was the mother of the famous hand surgeon Dr. Paul Brand, author of such classic Christian books as *In His Image* and *Fearfully and Wonderfully Made*. *Reader's Digest* even did a biography of him once because he revolutionized the treatment of leprosy in India and was eventually knighted by the queen of Great Britain. The Brands were British missionaries to India, but Mother Brand's husband died early on. So Mother Brand returned to England for a while, raised her two children, Paul and Mary, and then came back to India to continue her pioneer missionary work.

Her calling was to a group of Indians living in some hills in a very remote section of India—so remote that to get to her home, one had to take a train, then a bus, then a bullock cart, and then a horse. She was an amazing lady, so powerful in the hands of God. Every few months, she came down from the hills to Vellore to visit her son, who was teaching at the medical school as a professor of orthopedics. Upon arriving in town, she would send word to two or three girls to come and visit her. Because I was emerging as one of the women leaders in the Lord's work there among the students, she was kind enough to reach out and invite me. We would gather in her room, where she would talk to us and advise us and quote Scripture to us and kneel down and pray for each one of us, laying her hands on our heads. She was probably in her eighties at the time.

I remember she used to say, in her forceful British accent, "It hurts me—it *hurts* me—that we are not preaching the gospel at the medical hospital as we should." So she would spend much of her time sharing the gospel with patient after patient, for hour after hour. One time, she had fractured her leg, and her son had put her in a cast. But that did not stop her from sharing her faith. She would literally crawl from bed to bed, dragging her immobilized leg behind her, to share the gospel with every person who would listen. She inspired me, and I determined to do more to spread the gospel myself.

CHAPTER SIX
GET STARTED

Follow Me, and I will make you fishers of men.
JESUS CHRIST (MATTHEW 4:19)

Don't let yourself be overwhelmed. Just take things one step at a time.

Begin by understanding your two core objectives:

1. To obey the Great Commandments—love the Lord your God with all your heart, soul, mind, and strength, and love your neighbors as yourself (see Matthew 22:35-40; Mark 12:29-31).
2. To fulfill the Great Commission—share the gospel of Jesus Christ with the whole world and make disciples of every nation (see Matthew 28:18-20).

Important Questions

Keep things simple. Stay focused. Anything that doesn't help you accomplish these two core objectives should be eliminated.

Let's begin answering some of the immediate questions you may be asking.

How Many People Should I Work With?

We are reluctant to give you a specific answer to this question of numbers. That's really up to you and God. Scripture doesn't give a specific answer, so we won't either. That said, we are happy to offer some advice based on experience.

The bottom line for us is simple: do more by doing less and doing it better.

Don't overreach. Yes, Jesus discipled twelve men. But he was, after all, God incarnate. Yes, you should follow his model. But you should also take things one step at a time. Remember, as we mentioned earlier, Jesus invited individuals to follow him. *Then* he assembled them into a team and trained them as a team.

We encourage you, therefore, to begin by discipling one person with whom you can meet individually, one-on-one, at least once a week. Care for him like a member of your own family. Answer his questions. Teach him the basics of the faith. Give him assignments and projects, as we'll discuss shortly. Invest in him. Watch him grow and mature.

At the same time, keep praying for God to raise up others for you to meet with individually. When he answers your prayers, form a small discipleship group. Young believers learn a lot in a group setting. Questions asked by one are often similar to those being thought of by others. Growth by one often encourages and motivates the others. Seeing the mistakes and failures made by one can often be helpful for the others as they learn how to handle such troubles with grace, mercy, prayer, repentance, forgiveness, and restoration. As you build a team and meet with them regularly, we also recommend that you continue to meet with each member of the group one-on-one, once a week if possible, but at least once a month. Personal time is as vitally important as group time.

Don't let your group grow beyond what you can handle. Once a group gets too big, the interpersonal dynamic begins to break down, and it becomes difficult for you to truly invest in each one.

Go slow. Think small. Dig deep.

How Do I Ask Someone If He Would Like to Be Discipled?

Ask with humility.

The Lord Jesus Christ could go right up to a man and say, "Follow me," and that man would drop everything and follow. But Jesus was already the personification of love and humility. If you take such an approach, you might be received a little differently.

If you're a pastor, missionary, or ministry staff leader, don't underestimate the power of inviting a younger believer to meet with you. Young people are rarely invited to meet with those who are ahead of them in the faith. By definition, they look at you with great respect. They are watching you from a distance. They're curious about you. So when you ask one of these younger people if he's interested in being discipled, he will very likely be interested in meeting with you.

People who are hungry to know God better will often be eager to be invited into a small, intimate, in-depth discipleship group. People want to be chosen from the crowd and told that they have real potential to grow into a man after God's own heart and be used by God to accomplish something significant and eternal. Everyone wants someone to believe in them.

Here are a few suggestions for when you ask whether someone would like you to disciple him:

- **Explain why you're approaching him.** You've observed that he's faithful, available, and teachable. You've prayed about it, and you believe God is telling you to ask this person if he'd be interested in meeting together for prayer and encouragement.
- **Explain what you'd like to do together.** You will teach him about discipleship. You will help him study the Scriptures for himself. You will teach him to pray and see God answer his prayers powerfully and supernaturally. You will teach him to share his faith here at home and around the world. And you will equip him so that he can make disciples of his own. Plus, you'll have a lot of fun together along the way.
- **Explain what would be involved.** You might begin by setting a meeting once a week for two hours at a time. Perhaps it would work best on a weeknight. Or perhaps a Saturday morning would be best. There will be

homework, projects, and maybe even some trips. The key is to challenge and encourage his spiritual growth and maturity, not to overwhelm and discourage him. Together you can adjust the pace as you proceed.

- **Explain how long a commitment this would be.** We recommend setting a short, specific time frame to begin with—say three months. Again, don't overwhelm him or yourself. Take things one step at a time. Evaluate how things are going at the end of three months. Decide then whether to proceed and how. If things are going well and you both want to continue, set a new goal, a bit longer—say six months. Good relationships take time.

   One of your first lessons for him should be the principle of doing more by doing less and doing it better. Teach him not to say yes to opportunities that prevent him from making discipleship a priority.

   That said, be careful about "poaching" or "cherry-picking" from someone else's Bible study or ministry group. Don't cause confusion or hurt feelings. Be sensitive and careful how you tread.

- **Explain when you'd like to get started.** Ask him to pray about the commitment and get back to you. Don't rush him, and don't let him make a commitment on the spot. Make sure he really prays about it and is as committed to this relationship as you are. Ask him to feel free to call you and/or get together with more questions. Give him your phone number and e-mail address.

   These are small but important signs right from

the beginning that you are inviting him to do something special, something different, something important—and that it will involve a personal relationship with you. It will also help him understand that this is serious and worthy of his commitment.

If He Says Yes, How Do We Get Started? What Do We Do First?

The first thing to do is invite him over to your home. We strongly recommend having your main discipleship meetings at your own home—rather than at his home, the church, a restaurant, a coffee shop, or any other location—for several reasons.

Above all, meeting at your home allows you to begin modeling hospitality right away. When you invite a man into your home, you invite him into your life. He will learn more about you than you could possibly communicate at a "neutral place." There's nothing neutral about discipleship. It's not business; it's personal. So make it personal. Let him see your tastes in food and music and decor. Let him meet your family. Let him see the pictures on your walls, the mementos you have from school and work and various mission trips. Let him get a sense of your hobbies and what you like to read and where you like to travel.

Remember, this person is supposed to be following you as you follow Christ—you're not following him. Yes, you should visit his home soon and not be a stranger there. But for him to follow you, he must begin to know you. And believe us, he will know you far better and more quickly—and begin to sense your care and appreciation for him—by coming into your home than by almost any other way.

Second, we recommend cooking a meal for him—or helping your spouse cook a meal for him—every time he comes over. Don't order a pizza or other restaurant food if you can avoid it. A good rule of thumb when discipling singles is *not* to serve them pizza or pasta, as they're practically the only things some singles already eat. Let him come into a home that's (hopefully) relatively neat and clean and filled with the aromas of home cooking. Make your favorite meals. Find out what his favorite meals are, and make them. You could even invite him to come over early and help you cook, if he'd like.

Perhaps you live in a country or culture that naturally practices hospitality. Wonderful. Don't change a thing. But many who are reading this book have never truly experienced the art of biblical hospitality. Many Americans are never invited into the homes of their peers, much less their pastors. Many young people in the United States and Europe are never invited into the homes of older believers. They rarely cook for themselves, and they need real food. More importantly, they need the real love that home cooking signals.

Think of it this way: opening your home and cooking someone a homemade meal is one of the best ways in the twenty-first century to wash someone's feet.

Yes, hospitality is a sacrifice. It will cost you time and some money. But that's what servant leadership is all about. Discipleship isn't about head knowledge. It's about the heart. And if the way to a man's heart is through his stomach, don't start with his head.

But, you ask, what if this person lives some distance from

me, like twenty or thirty minutes away or more? Shouldn't I meet him at some halfway point between my home and his? Maybe. But we can't emphasize strongly enough how important it is to practice hospitality and have him at your home on a regular basis. Discipleship is best practiced in the context of the warmth and love and security of biblical hospitality. So make such hospitality a top priority. After all, in the New Testament, hospitality is not an option but a command.

- "Practice hospitality" (Romans 12:13, NIV).
- "Above all, keep fervent in your love for one another. . . . Be hospitable to one another without complaint" (1 Peter 4:8-9).
- "An overseer, then, must be above reproach . . . respectable, hospitable, able to teach" (1 Timothy 3:2).
- "The overseer must be above reproach as God's steward . . . hospitable, loving what is good" (Titus 1:7-8).

Okay, So I've Invited Him over to My Home. Now What?

Here are some practical suggestions to get started in discipleship.

TESTIMONIES

In your first meeting—even your first several meetings—we encourage you to ask this person to share his testimony, his own personal spiritual story of how he came to know Christ and what joys and challenges he's faced along the way. Share your testimony as well. This is not a time to begin teaching him everything you know. Now is the time to begin getting to know each other in a deeper and more personal way. Perhaps you have already heard his testimony, or he has heard yours. No matter. Share them again. Offer more detail and ask him to do the same so that you can both get a better, clearer sense of where God has brought you from and where he may be leading you.

Also, ask about his family. Where are they from? What are some things you can be praying about for his family? Do they know the Lord? Are they walking with the Lord? Are they in good health? Jesus healed Peter's mother-in-law. The least you can do is take a sincere interest in getting to know about your disciple's family and begin praying earnestly for them.

The key here is being a good listener. Be slow to speak and quick to listen. Ask questions that signal your interest in his life and future. Take notes that will help you remember what he says and that you can reread later when certain details become fuzzy. The better you listen, the more likely you are to begin convincing him that you care about him and that he can trust you. Very few adults listen to young people. Very few seem to care about what they think and what they've done (for good or ill) and what they dream. That's why so many young people feel so lonely and so isolated. Be different. Over the weeks and months ahead, truly convince this disciple of Jesus Christ that you love him.

SPIRITUAL ASSESSMENT

As you listen to the testimony of the person you are discipling, gently probe to assess the level and quality of his faith in Christ. To begin with, are you 100 percent sure he has given his life to Christ? Don't assume anything. Take the earliest opportunity to walk him through a gospel tract such as the "Four Spiritual Laws" or the "Bridge to Life" or something similar if you have even the *slightest* doubt that he is born again.

Here, a word of caution is in order. We fully understand that you don't want to offend this person the moment you've begun meeting with him by seeming to question whether he is a true believer in Jesus Christ, rather than just someone who is able to say the right words and use the right jargon. But few things could be worse than to misdiagnose his spiritual condition from the first day. You can't build where there is no foundation. The foundation must be rock-solid faith in the lordship of Jesus Christ. So *make sure*. This should not offend him. If he really doesn't know Christ but thinks he's a Christian, you're doing him a huge favor—helping him enter eternal salvation and avoid the fires of hell. If he does know Christ but is a little shaky on how to explain his salvation, then you're still doing him a huge favor by helping him get the basics of the faith established in his own heart and mind. Be especially careful not to be insensitive or rude. Just be kind and direct and clear. If he does become offended, explain your concerns in a calm and gentle and forthright way. If he is truly faithful, available, and teachable, this will be no problem.

Once you're sure he's born again—and that he has true biblical assurance of his salvation—begin assessing how spiritually mature he is.

- Does he have daily quiet times of Bible study and prayer?
- What book of the Bible is he studying?

- Is he really studying the Word, or is he just reading through a Christian book and not even realizing that, as wonderful as Christian books are, they are no substitute for time in God's holy Word?
- Does he understand basic biblical theology—the death and resurrection of Christ, the Trinity, the role and importance of the Holy Spirit, the biblical role of the church, the nature of sin and evil and spiritual warfare? Now is not the time to lead him through seminary. But you should try to get a sense of where he is—a benchmark of sorts—so you can prayerfully plan how to help him grow.

GOALS

Early on—probably in one of your first few meetings—ask the person you're working with to write down some of his personal goals and some of his goals for this relationship. Write down yours as well. If he doesn't have any goals yet for this new world of discipleship, that's okay. Talk it through with him, and begin to pray with him about what God wants for his life. Don't teach a person to be a strategist. Teach him, instead, to be a faithful servant, always looking to the Lord for wisdom and guidance and direction.

We recommend you give this quite a bit of prayer even before you get together. Don't wing it. Be fully prepared. You need to convince him by everything you say and do that you know where you're going. So seek the Lord. Ask him to reveal to you where he wants you to go and how he wants you to get there—and do this *before* you meet the person who wants to be discipled.

Make copies of his goals and yours and give each other a copy to keep. At the end of the first three months, it might be interesting to get them out, review them, and see what has happened and what may have changed.

PRAY TOGETHER

It is absolutely essential that you model a powerful prayer life right from the beginning of your ministry of making disciples. If you don't have a particularly strong prayer life, now is the time to start one, with your disciple helping keep you accountable and vice versa. Jesus prayed constantly—so much so that the disciples asked him to teach them how to pray.

Why focus so much on prayer? Because it is in prayer that we hide away and meet with God heart-to-heart. Prayer is where we quiet our souls and listen for his still, small voice directing us to wait or to go to the right or the left. Prayer is where we begin to discover the greatness of our great God, where we ask for miracles and he begins to answer.

So pray, pray, pray.

- Pray when you begin your meetings.
- Pray before you eat.
- Pray before you open the Word of God.
- Pray at length for *specific* prayer requests—yours and his.
- Pray for your church leaders and staff by name and for *specific* needs.
- Pray for missionaries and other workers by name and for *specific* needs.

- Pray for the Lord of the harvest to raise up more workers—from within your own church and within your own ministry—to serve the Lord in full-time vocational ministry or elsewhere.
- Pray for traveling mercies when one of you goes somewhere.
- Often—perhaps once a month—devote your entire meeting together to just getting on your knees in prayer. Believe God for the "small things." But also believe him for huge things. Ask him for big miracles, and keep a journal of your *specific* prayer requests so you can see how he answers your prayers. The more specific you are, the more clearly you will see God's answers to your prayers. In other words, rather than pray, "Lord, please bless my young friend, Bob," be specific. "Lord, please bless my young friend, Bob, by providing the five hundred dollars he needs to fix his car." Or, "Lord, please bless my friend, Bob, by opening the eyes of his sister and bringing her into a personal relationship with Jesus Christ."
- Finally, always be sure to rejoice together when you see prayers answered.

Remember, seeing God move in response to prayer is one way we discover the greatness of our great God—that he is a prayer-*hearing* God and a prayer-*answering* God.

Be careful not to take up your whole prayer time talking *about* your prayer requests. Jealously guard your actual prayer time, and don't let your teaching, your fellowship, your phone, or anything else intrude on it.

Make prayer your highest priority—and your constant practice—and you will set a powerful example. Believe us from years of experience: If you don't teach the person you're discipling to pray, who will? How will he learn? The truth is, he won't. Instead, he will think praying is something disciples talk about but never quite get around to. And nothing could be further from Jesus' example.

BIBLE STUDY

One of the critical keys to the success of your new relationship is helping the person you're investing in truly understand the Word of God and how to study it for himself. In part, this is so he can come to an accurate understanding of what spiritual reproduction is all about, why it's important, and how he can begin to grow to the point where he's spiritually mature enough to make disciples of his own.

It would be particularly helpful to teach him the inductive method of studying the Bible. For example, pick a passage of Scripture to study, and then approach it in three ways:

1. **Observation** (What does the passage actually say?)—Here, the goal is to be a reporter. You're looking for the facts, just the facts. Write down all the facts and details you can actually see in the text—the "who, what, when, where, why, and how" of the passage. Be very careful not to assume that words or phrases or ideas are there when they actually are not. The more carefully you observe the passage, the more you'll truly understand what God is specifically trying to tell you. For example, many

people read the Great Commission in Matthew 28:18-20 and believe it is about preaching the gospel to the whole world. It is certainly that—but it is much more, as well. Careful observation reveals that the passage is about both evangelism and *making disciples* of all nations, something too often overlooked or underappreciated. Only by observing the centrality of discipleship will people be able to accurately interpret the Great Commission, let alone apply it to their own lives. Teach people to be very, very careful about learning to observe Scripture accurately.

2. **Interpretation** (What does the passage mean?)— Here, the goal is to be a researcher. Search the Scriptures to find other passages that will help you understand the one you're studying. Look up other verses of Scripture that may be quoted in the passage in order to get a sense of the context. Look up any and all cross-references. Consider the history of the time and the context of events leading up to and surrounding the particular passage. Then, when you've carefully—and prayer-fully—considered the passage from all angles, you can begin to understand what the writer meant to say and what God was saying through him. For example, once you've studied the Great Commission in Matthew 28:18-20—who said it, whom it was said to, where it was said, why it was said, and how Jesus thought his listeners would understand what he said—the next step is to ask,

143

What was Jesus' point? What did he mean for his disciples to do as a result of what he was saying? Careful observation in this case leads to an accurate interpretation: Jesus told his disciples to make *more* disciples, for this is his strategy for reaching the whole world with his love and message.

3. **Application** (What does the passage mean to me?)— Here, the goal is to be a *doer*, not only a *hearer* of God's Word. Now that you know what the passage means, how does God want you to apply his truths to your own personal life? What are you supposed to do about what you've just learned? In the case of the Great Commission, this, too, is quite obvious once you've carefully observed and interpreted the passage. As a disciple of Jesus Christ, you are supposed to follow his command to help other believers understand and obey all that Jesus commanded and to help them grow to maturity so they can spiritually reproduce in the lives of others.

You can and should apply this inductive Bible study method to any passage of Scripture. Doing so on a regular basis with the person you're investing in will help him learn how to study the Word on his own.

It is absolutely essential that as you study the Scriptures together, you lay a firm, solid, biblically accurate theological foundation in the heart and mind of the one you're discipling. A person will never grow—and indeed may fall away and/or cause others to fall away from the faith—if he isn't grounded in solid biblical theology. To laymen, *theology* sounds like a big, intimidating word. *How am I supposed to teach theology?* you may be thinking. *I'm no seminary professor.*

Don't be anxious. If you're a solid Christian, you know more theology than you realize. We recommend getting a copy of your church's statement of faith and going through it together. If you're attending a good, Bible-believing church, the statement of faith will provide you with solid biblical theology and the Bible verses to back it up. This will help the person you're investing in a great deal—and you yourself may learn (or relearn) some important truths along the way.

There are also many Bible study guides and resources for helping new or ungrounded Christians get started in their faith available in the United States and globally over the Internet. Here are some excellent books and Bible studies to consider:

- *Discipleship Essentials: A Guide to Building Your Life in Christ* by Greg Ogden
- *Growing in Christ: A Thirteen-Week Follow-Up Course for New and Growing Christians* by the Navigators
- *The New How to Study Your Bible Workbook: Discover the Life-Changing Approach to God's Word* by Kay Arthur, David Arthur, and Pete De Lacy
- *Living By the Book: The Art and Science of Reading the Bible* by Howard Hendricks and William Hendricks
- *Experiencing God: Knowing and Doing the Will of God* by Henry Blackaby

Other good places to turn for such resources are ministries such as Cru (formerly known as Campus Crusade for

Christ), the Navigators, InterVarsity Christian Fellowship, the Billy Graham Evangelistic Association, Walk Thru the Bible, Moody Bible Institute, Operation Mobilization, the Southern Baptist Convention, Calvary Chapel and the ministry of Pastor Chuck Smith, Kay Arthur's Precept Ministries International, Dallas Theological Seminary, the ministry of Pastor Chuck Swindoll, and the ministry of Pastor John MacArthur.

Early on, you might consider using basic follow-up materials from these ministries to teach foundational concepts such as assurance of salvation, how to study the Bible, how to pray, the importance of the Spirit-filled life, and how to share your faith.

We also recommend that soon after you cover some of these foundational truths, you begin a weekly study together of one of the Gospels, concentrating specifically on how Jesus loved his heavenly Father, grew to maturity, developed the ability to communicate the gospel to anyone and everyone who would listen, and began discipling a small group of men hand-chosen by the Father.

Whatever you do, please don't study any book other than the Bible as the *centerpiece* of your time of discipleship. This book is at best a tool to help you learn the basic principles of discipleship and the invested life. Please use it as a complement, not a substitute, to teaching people the Word of God.

QUIET TIMES

Teach the person you're working with to study the Word and pray on his own, not just with you, for he will find true joy when hidden away alone with the Lord. Here are some suggestions:

- Encourage him to set a specific time each morning to get up and spend quiet time alone with the Lord. Urge him not to read the newspaper or turn on the television or read his e-mails or get involved in any other business before he spends time with the Lord. It is best to come to the Lord with a clear head and a fresh heart.

- Encourage him to find a quiet, private place to be with God, a place where he is unlikely to be disturbed or distracted—without phones ringing, without the TV or radio playing, and without people interrupting.

- Encourage him to begin by confessing his sins and asking the Lord to forgive him and purify him according to 1 John 1:9—"If we confess our sins, He is faithful and righteous to forgive us our sins and to cleanse us from all unrighteousness." Encourage him as well to remember David's plea to God in Psalm 51—"Wash me, and I shall be whiter than snow. Make me to hear joy and gladness. . . . Create in me a clean heart, O God, and renew a steadfast spirit within me. Do not cast me away from Your presence and do not take Your Holy Spirit from me. Restore to me the joy of Your salvation and sustain me with a willing spirit. Then I will teach transgressors Your ways, and sinners will be converted to You." First come confession and purity. Then comes joy. Then come evangelism and discipleship.

- Encourage him to worship the Lord in spirit and truth. (See more in chapter 8, "Worship Together.")

- Encourage him to ask God each morning to truly be the Lord and Master of his life. To be on the throne of his life. To be in the driver's seat of his life. To fill him continually with his Holy Spirit to lead, guide, and direct him in the way that he should go. "Be [continually] filled with the Spirit," we read in Ephesians 5:18. "Walk by the Spirit," we read in Galatians 5:16. "Worship in spirit and truth," we read in John 4:24.

- Remind him that disciples cannot live the Christian life in their own strength and power; it is foolish to try. That's why Jesus told his disciples, "I will ask the Father, and He will give you another Helper, that He may be with you forever. . . . The Helper, the Holy Spirit, whom the Father will send in My name, He will teach you all things, and bring to your remembrance all that I said to you" (John 14:16, 26). For it is the Holy Spirit—not you—that will develop Christlike character (the "fruit of the Spirit") in the lives of the people you are discipling, according to Galatians 5:16-25. And it is the gifts of the Spirit (Romans 12:6-8; 1 Corinthians 12–14; Ephesians 4:11-16) that God gives us "for the equipping of the saints for the work of service, to the building up of the body of Christ" (Ephesians 4:12).

- Encourage him to pray the psalmist's prayer from Psalm 119:18—"Open my eyes, that I may behold wonderful things from Your law."

- Encourage him to prayerfully and systematically study a specific book of the Bible (perhaps one you're studying together). Roaming aimlessly through the

Scriptures from day to day is not a good way to grow spiritually. The Gospel according to John might be a good place to start, as he will learn about the person of Jesus Christ through the eyes of one of his most trusted disciples. Reading a psalm or a chapter in Proverbs before bed at night is a good habit. It is also a good idea to begin reading the Bible from Genesis through Revelation during daily quiet time.

- Encourage him not to try to cover too many verses at one time but instead to observe, interpret, apply, and meditate on a few verses that really stand out to him. By meditating on such verses, we mean thinking about them over and over, praying about what they mean, asking God to reveal every nuance, and in the process coming to know such verses so well that they are committed to memory. Like a cow chewing its cud, so we should chew on God's Word.

    - "How sweet are Your words to my taste! Yes, sweeter than honey to my mouth!" (Psalm 119:103)

    - "O taste and see that the LORD is good; how blessed is the man who takes refuge in Him!" (Psalm 34:8)

    - "This book of the law shall not depart from your mouth, but you shall meditate on it day and night, so that you may be careful to do all that is written in it; for then you will make your way prosperous, and then you will have success" (Joshua 1:8).

- Encourage him to keep a personal prayer journal and be specific both about his prayers and about God's answers (which include yes, no, and wait).
- Encourage him to specifically ask the Lord to lead, guide, and direct his steps throughout the day, in small decisions and in large. Encourage him to pray Proverbs 3:5-6 in order to trust in the Lord with all his heart and not lean on his own understanding. Also, encourage him to ask the Lord to show him someone to whom he may show love and compassion and the gospel that very day.
- Encourage him to steadily carve out more time for the Lord. Ideally, he would spend at least forty-five minutes to an hour with the Lord before he begins his day. Many faithful servants spend much more time. But this is a good goal to aim for.

    Don't let him be confused by *quality* time versus *quantity* time. The Lord deserves—and you and the person you're investing in need—both quality and quantity time. Yes, he probably is a busy person. So was Jesus. So was Paul. But they made time alone with their Father in heaven their top priority. "In the early morning, while it was still dark, Jesus got up, left the house, and went away to a secluded place, and was praying there" (Mark 1:35).
- Finally, keep him accountable. Ask him regularly if he is having his quiet time, what he is studying, what he is learning, what God is asking him to apply, and what prayers he is seeing answered. You may even want to e-mail or text each other every day after you've

finished your quiet times as a way to keep each other accountable and to share with each other a verse you found encouraging and prayer requests that are on your hearts.

BAPTISM

According to the Lord Jesus' words in Matthew 28:19, the first task in the art of making disciples is "baptizing them in the name of the Father and the Son and the Holy Spirit." It's all part of "teaching them to observe [obey] all that I commanded you" (v. 20).

Ask the person you're investing in if he has ever been baptized by immersion since giving his life to Jesus Christ (not as an infant). If so, ask him to tell you about his baptism, why he did it, where, what it meant to him, and why he would encourage other new and young believers to be baptized as well. If he was truly born again before being baptized, there is no need for him to be baptized again. Indeed, there is no biblical example of being baptized more than once, so we should not encourage multiple baptisms. It is not like the taking of communion that is done often. One baptism is sufficient. That's the biblical model.

That said, if he's never been baptized, take the opportunity to walk him through Scriptures explaining what baptism is, why it's important, and why if Jesus pleased his Father by being baptized, we should do no less. Then, when you complete a study like this, encourage him to be baptized as soon as possible.

Your disciple's willingness to follow the example and command of Jesus by being baptized is the first real test of his teachability. It is also the first test of your commitment as a leader, whether or not you are willing to baptize people just as Jesus commands in the Great Commission. Don't be surprised if the whole concept is new to him or if he suddenly experiences strong spiritual resistance. Baptism looks so simple to mature Christians. Indeed, it is a very simple act. But it is hugely significant.

If the person you're working with is nervous or resistant, it is because he intuitively understands the enormous spiritual significance of publicly identifying with the death, burial, and resurrection of Jesus Christ. So don't force him to be baptized that night or that week. But don't forget the issue either. Invest some time in this, gently answering the disciple's questions and addressing his fears. Pray for him. Pray with him. But don't go too long without making sure he is baptized. If he isn't willing to obey at this first and critical juncture, he isn't ready to go any further.

At one end of the spectrum, some churches put an enormous emphasis on baptism, even going to the point of saying a person cannot be saved unless he is baptized. But Scripture doesn't teach us that baptism is necessary for salvation. The thief on the cross who believed on the Lord Jesus didn't have a chance to be baptized, yet the Lord said, "Today you shall be with Me in Paradise" (Luke 23:39-43). At the other end of the spectrum, some churches put very little emphasis on baptism, even going to the point of acting as though baptism is of little or no importance for believers. But that's not true either. Baptism isn't necessary for salvation, but it is necessary as an act of obedience once a person is saved.

Here are a few examples from Scripture of the importance of baptism:

- Jesus was baptized in obedience, thus pleasing his Father (Luke 3:21-22).
- Jesus commanded his disciples to baptize new believers (Matthew 28:18-20).
- Peter told new believers in Jesus to "repent, and . . . be baptized," and they obeyed (Acts 2:38-41).
- When Philip preached the gospel, people repented and were baptized (Acts 8:12).
- When Paul received Christ, he was baptized (Acts 9:18).
- When the Roman jailer was saved, he immediately was baptized (Acts 16:33).
- Paul teaches us that baptism is a symbol of identifying with Christ's death (we are buried in water as he was buried in the ground) and resurrection (we come up out of the water as he came up from the grave) (Romans 6:2-4).

QUESTIONS

1. Write down some of the small, manageable tasks you need to complete as you get started making a disciple.

2. What are some of your goals for this new relationship? Examples should include spiritual/discipleship goals but may also include family goals, professional goals, health/fitness goals, etc.

3. What book of the Bible are you going to begin studying verse by verse, chapter by chapter? What are some of the things the Lord is teaching you through this portion of Scripture?

4. Why is baptism important? Why isn't baptism essential for salvation?

5. Why was Jesus baptized? Why was Paul baptized?

TESTIMONY: MARRIAGE
MRS. INDIRA KOSHY, MD

While Koshy was a student at Syracuse University, he was opening his tiny bachelor's apartment each week for international students to come over, eat, make friends, and have conversations about Christ.

When Koshy and I became engaged, I moved from India to Syracuse. The hospital that hired me graciously gave me a small apartment when I first arrived. But we would need more space when we got married, which at that point was only five months away. So we started looking all over Syracuse for something that would meet our needs. The Lord has said he will provide for our every need, so we took him at his word.

Koshy prayed specifically for three things.

First, the apartment needed to be close to campus so students could get there easily.

Second, it needed a large living room so we could show hospitality to more students.

Third, it needed to be strategically located so every foreign student would know where it was.

It was a great prayer. There was just one problem: with some twenty-four thousand students signed up for fall classes, we simply couldn't find anything near campus, much less large enough for the ministry.

That's when a priceless Christian couple named James and Elsie Hyslop came to visit us from Ohio. Mr. Hyslop was a dear friend of Koshy's and the president of a coal company, and he had adopted Koshy like his own son. They had been introduced to each other by one of Koshy's Bible college professors. The Hyslops knew we were hunting for an apartment and finding it difficult, and the wedding was quickly approaching. But we weren't really worried. We knew the Lord would provide. And he did.

One day during their visit, Mr. Hyslop turned to us and said, "I would like to buy you a house." We were both stunned, so stunned that Koshy immediately turned down the offer. Logically he had a good reason. He thought we would be leaving the States after he finished his master's degree program the following year. We didn't want to own anything. We just needed a good apartment.

So the Hyslops went back to Ohio. We kept looking. But we found nothing. Time was running short. We kept praying. Finally Koshy called Mr. Hyslop, whom he called "Dad," and asked if his offer was still good.

"Absolutely, Koshy. You two pick out any house you'd like. Money is no object."

Breathless at the greatness of our great God, we set out with our real estate agent to find the perfect house. But we couldn't find any good houses close enough to campus. So a few weeks later, we picked out the best we could, though it didn't meet any of the three conditions Koshy had prayed about, and called Mr. Hyslop. His mother was sick, but he said, "Koshy, I'll be there tomorrow."

He flew in, and we showed him the house we had selected. None of us were really satisfied, and Mr. Hyslop insisted that there must be something better. So he asked our real estate agent to find something closer.

"Well, you know," the agent replied, "last night as I was leaving the office, the telephone rang and a woman said her house was going on the market near campus. It's not officially on the market yet, but would you like to go see it?"

Absolutely. We all raced over to the house immediately. My friends, if it had not happened to me, I'm not sure I would have believed it. But even without going inside, Koshy and I looked at each other and said, "This is the house!"

First of all, it was just one block from campus. Second, it was huge. Third, S.U.'s international student office was on the corner of the very same street, so every international student would know that street. It was a total miracle. All three conditions of Koshy's prayer were met. We were on cloud nine.

"Do you like this house?" Mr. Hyslop asked. But just by looking at us, he knew our answer. He immediately wrote out a check for the down payment. He didn't even bargain the price down. The house was spick-and-span. There was a beautiful green-and-white awning and a matching swing.

It was by far the best of all the houses we saw—and we had originally set out looking for an apartment.

But there was more.

The woman who lived there became excited that we were getting married and that this was going to be our first home. She and her husband were being transferred and didn't want to transport lots of boxes or furniture. So she offered us most of their mahogany furniture, appliances, curtains, rugs, and dishes—even many of the antiques in their basement.

"Whatever you don't want, you leave it and I'll buy it for them," Mr. Hyslop said.

So they did. We were in business right away. On September 28—Koshy's birthday—we closed on the house. I moved in immediately to get it ready. We were married on October 14. Once again, we were seeing the greatness of our great God in action, and we simply had to fall on our knees to praise and worship him.

The great thing was that Koshy and I both had such a burden to win souls—especially students—that being married and serving together felt very natural. In college, I used to say I didn't want to get married because how could I find a husband who would let me have students in my house all the time? Now the Lord had given me a husband with the exact same calling: friendship evangelism and discipleship.

Every other weekday night, we would have twenty-five to thirty foreign students over to our home to have a meal and make some friends and talk about Christ. We developed our little system. I worked in the hospital during the day. Koshy worked on his master's degree and invited students to dinner. He would buy the groceries, chop the vegetables, prepare the chicken, and get everything ready. I would come home about five o'clock and start cooking. We were both very fast, and we were having fun serving the Lord together. The students, mostly unbelievers, would start arriving around 6:30 p.m. We would serve buffet style, with everyone sitting everywhere— in the dining room and living room and kitchen. Afterward, Koshy would talk with the men. The young women would help me with the dishes while we talked about the Lord, and I would answer their many questions.

It would have been easy to get overwhelmed very quickly. But just as the Lord supernaturally provided us a home and the financial resources to serve him, he also supernaturally provided wonderful friends with servants' hearts to come help us do his work.

Our first great blessing in that regard was Rosemary Hyslop, the daughter of the couple who bought us our home. About a year younger than me, she contacted us during our first year of marriage and ministry and said she wanted to work with the students. So in 1968 she came to live with us. She taught in the nursing school during the day and helped us in the evenings and on weekends. Later, she resigned her job and worked with us full-time. She shopped for the groceries and did the house cleaning. She helped do the cooking. She invited women for meals and visited them in the dorms. She took women shopping and invested long hours with them in Bible study and prayer. What a blessing.

Over time, many other women have come to help us, and I've had the privilege of working side by side with them, discovering together the joy of biblical hospitality and friendship evangelism. My sister Usha came to work with us for many years, as did my other sister, Renu, which was so much fun. A wonderful young woman named Annie Chandy came and actually lived with us for eight years before she got married, learning the Word, praying with us, and helping us serve the students. A sweet young woman named Rita Kapadia came for a weekend and stayed two years. Even my mother, Dinah Perry, came to live with us for many years until she went home to be with the Lord. She was a wonderful blessing, to us and to the students, and I'm so glad for every moment she was here. There have been many others, different people at different times, for whom I have been so grateful. Without them I'm not sure how we would have managed.

For Christian women, hospitality is such an important and fun ministry. Many people feel as if they don't know how to "disciple" someone. It sounds so daunting at first. But any woman can open her home and have a little dinner party. The secret is praying faithfully for the Lord to guide and direct you and to bless those who come over to your home.

CHAPTER SEVEN

GO DEEPER

> *. . . teaching them to observe all that I*
> *commanded you . . .*
>
> JESUS CHRIST (MATTHEW 28:20)

Once you've begun to meet regularly—one-on-one—ask God to bring others along whom you can also invest in and who can form a small discipleship group.

As God answers, gather your new team together for prayer and worship, Bible study, and ministry training.

Begin by giving each person an opportunity to share his testimony with the others so you can really get to know one another.

As we've seen, Jesus invited individuals to follow him, but he discipled and trained a team.

You should do the same.

Concentrate on establishing the basics of the faith in each person and in the team as a whole. Again, your job is not to give them a seminary education. But it is essential that they become workmen who are unashamed of the gospel, able to accurately handle the Word of Truth and willing to obey everything Jesus has commanded.

To this end, work on developing the seven habits of a highly effective disciple.

A highly effective disciple is one who

1. is devoted to consistent, continual, passionate, supernatural prayer (Colossians 4:2-4);
2. is engaged in a consistent, daily, disciplined study of God's Word (Acts 17:11);
3. actively participates in a Bible-believing local church that baptizes new believers, teaches the Word, serves Communion, gathers for prayer, praise, and worship, and enjoys Christian fellowship (Acts 1–2);
4. is committed to obeying and integrating God's Word in every area of life and thus bearing the fruit of the Spirit, the fruit of changed character (Galatians 5:22-25);
5. develops his spiritual gifts and uses those gifts to serve others and build up the body of Christ (Romans 12:1-8; Ephesians 4:11-16; 1 Corinthians 12–14);
6. makes the most of every opportunity to share the gospel of Jesus Christ in a genuine, sincere, and effective manner with those in every culture who seek a personal relationship with God (Colossians 4:5-6); and
7. takes younger believers under his wing to train them up in the way they should go and "make disciples of all the nations" (Matthew 28:18-20).

Don't get nervous. It's God's responsibility—not yours—to develop this Christlikeness in those you're investing in. Your job is to help. These are simply guidelines to help you know what you're aiming at. And the job won't get done in three months or six or a year or even three. It's a lifelong process we're talking about here, and this is just the beginning.

So take a deep breath and relax.

That said, don't be afraid to challenge your team.

Every time you come to a command of Jesus during your study of one of the Gospels, hunker down on that point. Talk about how each of you can put that verse into practice. Even if it's difficult. *Especially* if it's difficult. Jesus didn't promise discipleship would be easy. Just the opposite. He said anyone who won't pick up his cross, die to himself, and follow Christ no matter what the cost isn't worthy of calling himself a disciple.

Be gentle with your team. Be patient with them. But don't soft-pedal, sidestep, sugarcoat, or skip over any of the commands of Jesus Christ as you move through the Scriptures. You do your team no favors. Instead, you communicate the exact opposite of true discipleship: that it's okay to be a hearer rather than a doer of God's Word. Nothing could be further from the truth, and nothing could be more damaging to their faith—and yours—than such an approach.

The Importance of Fellowship

As you study the Gospels and get to verses about the role of the church—say Matthew 16:18, where Jesus renames Simon, calling him Peter, and says, "Upon this rock I will build My church"—have a candid conversation about how important Christian fellowship is to the life and health of every believer.

Show your team Acts 2:42—indeed, all of chapter 2— where we see how central fellowship is to the lives of healthy disciples and healthy churches.

Explain to your team how to find a good church, how to find a good Bible study, and how to find good Christian friends to pray with and study with and do life with. Explain to them why you attend the church you do. Explain the importance of fellowship in your own life. And explain to them the difference between getting together with Christian friends—which is fine—and real fellowship, which is far better. Strong believers will truly encourage each other "to love and good deeds" (Hebrews 10:24), to grow and stretch and press forward in their faith, not stagnate or wallow where they are. Talk to them about the vibrancy of Christian community as found in Acts 2.

At the same time, warn them about the perils of falling out of real Christian fellowship. We have personally seen some of the most tragic—and unexpected—casualties of the faith come when believers slowly get "too busy" for God, for his Word, and for his people. Such believers develop a habit of not spending time with other believers, of drifting from God's people, and in turn developing a callousness toward the things of God. Soon they have given Satan a foothold and may suddenly find themselves living in great sin, often shocking and deeply grieving friends and loved ones.

Warn your team to be on their guard for signs of their own drifting. Warn them to be on guard for their friends and family members too, for signs that *they* are drifting from fellowship and from the Lord. Warn them not to miss or skip church or Bible study except under rare and specific circumstances.

Point them to Hebrews 10:24-25, where the writer says, "Let us consider how to stimulate one another to love and good deeds, not forsaking our own assembling together, as is the habit of some, but encouraging one another; and all the more as you see the day drawing near."

After all, being a disciple means developing discipline— and discipline means going to church or Bible study even when you don't feel like it. Don't let them get in the habit of skipping time with God's people, as some do. Instead, help them develop the habit of holiness, starting with the fellowship of a warm, loving, caring Christian community.

Most important, don't just talk about fellowship, but model the importance of warm Christian fellowship. Here are some ideas:

- Go out to dinner together as a group.
- Go hiking or camping together.
- Go running or exercising together.
- Go to a Christian conference together.
- Go to a sporting event or a concert together.
- Plan and do a ministry project together.
- Plan and take a mission trip together.
- Go to a park or a crowded public place and practice sharing the gospel together.
- Plan and host an evangelistic block party or vacation Bible school together in your neighborhood.
- Plan events that will raise money for missionaries or the needy in your own church.

These are just a few suggestions. We're sure you'll have many more ideas. The key is to "go ye therefore." Don't become "spiritual couch potatoes." Practice what you preach. Be active—and enjoy your time together. That's how your disciples will truly understand what fellowship is really all about.

The Importance of Tithing and Giving

As you study the Gospels and you get to verses about tithing and sacrificial giving of the resources God has so generously given you and your team—Matthew 6:1-4, for example— have a candid conversation about what that means and why God wants us to invest financially in his Kingdom.

Explain to your team the way you tithe and give, that your tithe should first go to the local church, and how you decided which individuals and ministries other than your local church God has directed you to support. Help your team develop a specific action plan for tithing and giving.

Will it be easy? Maybe not. Will people naturally want to give 10 percent of their gross income—or more—to the Lord if they're not already doing so? Maybe not. Where is their heart, their treasure? Is their primary love God or mammon (money and material possessions)? Spend some time studying Matthew 6:19-34 together.

Teach your team the parable of the talents, found in Matthew 25:14-30. Teach them what spiritual investing is all about.

Teach them what God says in Malachi 3:10: "'Bring the whole tithe into the storehouse, so that there may be food in

My house, and test Me now in this,' says the LORD of hosts, 'if I will not open for you the windows of heaven and pour out for you a blessing until it overflows.'"

Handling money as a wise steward is a big part of being a true disciple. Talking about money really gets to the core of where a man's heart is.

Again, be gentle and patient, but also be candid and firm. If this is a difficult area for you as well, then get down on your knees and plead with the Lord to give you the strength to set a new course and to be a bold example. If you're going to tell people, "Follow me," then you must be headed in the right direction.

The Importance of Sexual Purity

Likewise, when you arrive at a Scripture such as Matthew 5:28, about the importance of being pure in heart and fleeing youthful lusts so as to not commit adultery, linger on that point. Talk about how each of you can put that verse into practice. Even though it's difficult. *Especially* because it's difficult.

Take your team through what the Bible has to say about lust (for example, Proverbs 6–7; Galatians 5:16; 2 Timothy 2:22; James 1:14-15; 4:1-2; 1 Peter 2:11; 1 John 2:16).

With men, show them Psalm 119:9 and 11—"How can a young man keep his way pure? By keeping it according to Your word. . . . Your word I have treasured in my heart, that I may not sin against You." Show them Job 31:1 and 4—"I made a covenant with my eyes not to look lustfully at a young woman. . . . Does he [God] not see my ways and count my every step?" (NIV).

With women, show them Proverbs 31 and 1 Timothy 2:9-10, and talk to them about the importance of dressing modestly and respectfully so as not to displease the Lord.

Talk about specific steps you can take to honor the Lord in these areas.

Be specific, personal, and confidential with each of your team members.

Are they having extramarital sexual relations? Are they engaged in unbiblical physical affection or otherwise inappropriate sexual behavior? You need to ask. You need to teach them God's disapproval of such behavior and help them stop and begin living a holy life.

You need to talk with them about the need to "abstain from all appearance of evil"—living in such a way that no one can even think or accuse them of doing something ungodly—just as Paul instructed in 1 Thessalonians 5:22 (KJV).

You need to talk to them about learning to live "above reproach"—living in such a way that nothing they do could even remotely cause their lives or faith to be disgraced or discredited or discounted because their behavior looks improper or ungodly—as Paul instructed in 1 Timothy 5:7.

Help men become known in their community as men of honor, men who so value and respect the reputation of the women they are courting that they would never do anything that could even possibly embarrass or discredit such women in the eyes of God or man.

Help women become known in their community as women of honor, women whose character, behavior, kindness, and sincere love for people set them apart as true disciples of Jesus Christ.

Moreover, talk about the role and mission and challenges of singleness and marriage from both a scriptural and a personal perspective. Be as candid as you can about your own convictions, struggles, and successes. If you're married, help your team see the joy of a godly marriage and understand why it's worthwhile to overcome every temptation that singles face.

Don't share inappropriate information. Don't betray the trust and confidence of your spouse or people with whom you've had previous relationships. Also, be careful not to give so much detail about moral failures you've experienced that you end up glorifying sin rather than glorifying God, perhaps even inciting temptation and lust rather than offering a strategy to defeat them. The key is to help your team set biblical goals for their lives, resist temptation, and avoid every sin and every appearance of sin.

Will such conversations be easy? Maybe not.

Will your team feel they are suddenly in over their heads, that you're trying to control their lives and become the "morality police" or "relationship police"? Perhaps.

So be gentle. Be kind. Be patient. But don't skirt or sidestep such issues. Be candid and helpful. These areas of life are as big as they are important. They should be handled with care, especially in fairly new relationships with your disciples. But they must be handled. Indeed, if you as a discipler don't help these younger men deal biblically and practically and positively with these issues and similar ones, who will?

Remember, your mandate as a discipler is to teach people not simply to *know* biblical facts but to *obey* everything the

Lord Jesus Christ commanded in Scripture. That's why your challenge is to be as practical as possible, minimizing pie-in-the-sky, fuzzy, big-picture talk and instead helping them discover specific ways to pursue holiness and avoid sin. Such work should be the role of godly fathers. But so few younger believers have godly fathers in our world today. Thus, the discipler must be prepared to help young people apply the Bible in every area of life.

The Importance of Long-Suffering

As you come across verses about pain and suffering as a believer in Jesus Christ—say Matthew 10:16-39 or the book of 1 Peter—focus on such verses. It is not a pleasant topic, but rejection, abuse, revilement, and even death are part of the disciple's life. There is no way of getting around that. So study what the Lord has to say in his Word about suffering, and study what he says about how to handle these attacks and these attackers.

Some pain will come by way of direct physical attacks by Satan, just as Job suffered. Some will come by way of physical attacks on family members and/or loved ones.

Some pain will come by way of emotional attacks, people mistreating and rejecting and ignoring and betraying you and those you are discipling, just as Jesus suffered—even from some of his own disciples.

Some pain will come by direct persecution, specifically because you are standing up for the precious name of Jesus. Disciples in some countries suffer far more than those in other countries. But the apostle Paul told Timothy that "all who desire to live godly in Christ Jesus will be persecuted" (2 Timothy 3:12). Not *might* be. Not *could* be. *Will* be. That's sobering—but that's reality. So prepare your team for what lies ahead.

Walk them through the book of Acts, observing that the believers handled suffering and rejection and loneliness and persecution with great patience and joy—and much, much prayer.

Study the wise words of Peter, who wrote, "Beloved, do not be surprised at the fiery ordeal among you, which comes upon you for your testing, as though some strange thing were happening to you; but to the degree that you share the sufferings of Christ, keep on rejoicing, so that also at the revelation of His glory you may rejoice with exultation" (1 Peter 4:12-13).

Walk them through the story of Revelation, keeping their eyes fixed on the ultimate goal, on being with Jesus and worshiping him with multitudes of disciples from every nation, tribe, and tongue. When we keep our eyes on Jesus—what he suffered willingly and what he's preparing for us joyfully—we can make it through any times of pain or persecution that come our way.

Here are some other specific ways you can model the importance of identifying with and caring for those brothers and sisters who are suffering around the world:

- Together, plan and host an all-night prayer vigil for the suffering church.
- Raise money to send to persecuted believers around the world.

- Plan and take a mission trip to serve a suffering church somewhere in the world.
- Raise money to rescue a persecuted pastor or national worker out of his country to go to a safer, freer country where he can be loved and encouraged and receive training and support.

The Importance of Spiritual Leadership

At the heart of biblical discipleship is the goal of helping disciples—spiritual *followers*—become disciple makers—spiritual *leaders*.

We are trying to help people experience God in a real and personal and powerful way. A large part of that means bringing them to a point of maturity and completeness and balance in all areas of their lives so that they are fully equipped to lead others closer to the Savior. That's what spiritual reproduction is all about.

A discipler makes it clear by what he says and by the way he lives that a good leader is not a mere "manager" or a "facilitator." Spiritual leadership is about something far more important.

Dr. Howard Hendricks, the renowned professor of Christian education at Dallas Theological Seminary, whom we mentioned earlier in this book, offers a good working definition of a leader, with two fundamental points:

1. A leader is one who knows where he or she is going and is going to the right place.
2. A leader is one who is able to persuade others to follow.

Some people, Dr. Hendricks points out, are gifted at stirring up a following but have no idea where they are going. Other people know precisely where they are going and are going to the right place. But they can't persuade anyone to go along with them. A good leader, a true leader, has both qualities. So must good disciplers.

The first element, Hendricks says, is conceptual. A strong Christian leader has a vision, a mission, and a destiny. He is deeply infected with a cause—a godly cause—and he wants to share it with others.

The second element is relational. The Christian leader not only has a cause. He also has a heart. He cares deeply for those he is discipling. He's constantly seeking ways to serve them, build them up, and meet their needs. In turn, he motivates them to love Christ and love others wholeheartedly.

This was the way Paul led men. In his first letter to the church at Thessalonica, Paul reminded those he had discipled that neither he nor his ministry team sought "glory from men . . . even though as apostles of Christ we might have asserted our authority."

Instead, he said, "We proved to be gentle among you, as a nursing mother tenderly cares for her own children. Having so fond an affection for you, we were well-pleased to impart to you not only the gospel of God but also our own lives, because you had become very dear to us. . . . You know how we were exhorting and encouraging and imploring each one of you as a father would his own children, so that you would walk in a manner worthy of the God who calls you into His own kingdom and glory" (1 Thessalonians 2:6-8, 11-12).

Of course Paul had a mission—a mission to communicate

the gospel of Jesus Christ to everyone who would listen. He knew where he was going. But he also loved the people with whom he was trying to communicate. He understood how to persuade people. Sometimes he cared for them as a tender, gentle mother. At other times he challenged, encouraged, and implored them as a strong father. Why? To convince them to live lives worthy of the God who loved them and gave himself for them. This balance must be our approach as well.

The Importance of Spiritual Gifts

A spiritual gift is not a natural talent or skill, like singing or writing or cooking well. It is the ability to touch and help change people's lives with supernatural effectiveness, using the tools of God's Word and God's love.

Let's look at spiritual gifts, as Paul describes them in three key passages of Scripture.

Spiritual Gifts in Ephesians 4:7-16

- **Apostles**—In the first century, these were personal eyewitnesses to—and personal ambassadors of— Jesus Christ to the world, specifically called by God to write the Scriptures, launch the church, and establish it among the nations. Thus, the specific gift of apostleship was unique to the twelve men Jesus trained—plus Paul and a few others mentioned in Scripture—and the canon of Scripture, of course, is closed. While today God no longer gives the gift of apostleship in the same way as he did in the first century, he certainly equips people in the power of the

Holy Spirit to be bold, pioneering missionaries and church planters with supernatural effectiveness.

· **Prophets**—Historically, a prophet was a "foreteller," speaking the Word of God through prophecy with supernatural revelations of God's plans and purposes for the future, in part to call people to repentance. A prophet was also a "forthteller," speaking forth the words God had already spoken to preach, teach, encourage, comfort, and inspire the people to repent and walk with the Lord. Again, to be clear, the canon of Scripture is closed, so God is not using the gift of prophecy today to write new portions of the Bible. Today we would call a person with the gift of prophecy a preacher, a "public expounder" of the Holy Scriptures. He is a person who can speak a message from God as revealed in the Bible with supernatural impact in a way that really motivates people to follow God. He also has the ability to teach prophecies already found in the Bible to contemporary audiences with supernatural clarity and insight, helping people understand what the ancient biblical prophecies say, what they mean, how they are relevant to current times, and to call people to repentance, holiness, and service to Christ.

· **Evangelists**—While not everyone has the gift of evangelism, all of us are, of course, called to share the gospel message of salvation through Jesus Christ to all men everywhere. That said, God has given some people the spiritual gift of being evangelists. They have the calling, duty, passion, and ability to share

the gospel in the power of the Holy Spirit and exhibit
supernatural effectiveness, bearing much fruit.

- **Pastors**—Not everyone who has this title necessarily
  has this gift. But those who do are people whom God
  has called and equipped to serve as "shepherds," able
  to guide, care for, correct, and lead a spiritual flock
  with supernatural compassion and effectiveness.
- **Teachers**—These are people whom God has called and
  equipped with the supernatural ability to understand
  and explain God's Word and God's ways in a way that
  cuts through to people's hearts and supernaturally
  motivates them to follow and obey Jesus Christ.

Spiritual Gifts in Romans 12:1-8

- **Prophecy**—See above.
- **Service**—The person with this gift is a person with the
  ability to care for people, wait upon them, and meet
  their needs with supernatural levels of compassion,
  hard work, and dedication.
- **Teaching**—See above.
- **Exhortation**—The person with this gift has the God-
  given ability to challenge, encourage, beseech, comfort,
  and admonish people in a way that supernaturally
  motivates them to make specific changes in their lives
  and live more fully and faithfully for Christ.
- **Giving** "with liberality"—The person with this gift is
  a person with the supernatural motivation to invest his
  time, talent, and treasure far above and beyond simple
  tithing. He loves to pour the resources God has given
  him into the Lord's eternal work.

- **Leading** "with diligence"—The person with this gift is not necessarily a person with natural leadership talent or natural charisma. But it is a person with a supernatural vision of what God wants him to do and who has the supernatural ability to persuade others to follow in pursuit of obeying the Great Commandments and fulfilling the Great Commission.
- **Mercy** "with cheerfulness"—The person with this gift displays a supernatural degree of compassion, joy, and optimism toward financially poor or otherwise needy people.

Spiritual Gifts in 1 Corinthians 12

Paul says that "concerning spiritual gifts . . . I do not want you to be unaware."

- **Wisdom**—This is the supernatural ability to understand with great clarity God's principles and precepts and to offer insightful guidance to others during times of difficult decision making.
- **Knowledge**—This is the supernatural ability to understand and retain information God finds useful to advancing his Kingdom, whatever the subject.
- **Faith**—All of us must have faith, a trust that God will do what he says and will reward those who earnestly seek him, for this is what pleases God (Hebrews 11:6). But some people have a supernatural ability to trust him to provide for their spiritual, physical, financial, and emotional needs—and the needs of others—in

a way that is a great testimony to other people of the greatness of our great God.

- **Healing**—This is the supernatural ability to heal a person's physical ailment through the power of Jesus Christ.
- **Miraculous Powers**—This is the ability to ask God to do supernatural events, and God does them.
- **Discernment (sometimes translated "distinguishing of spirits")**—This is supernatural insight given by the Holy Spirit to read a person or situation and to understand in a God-given way what is really going on and why, often before other believers fully see or understand the situation themselves.
- **Ability to Speak in Different Kinds of Tongues**— There is great controversy over this gift. Some believe it is the supernatural ability to speak in foreign languages, while others believe it is the ability to speak in a language that only God knows.
- **Ability to Interpret Different Kinds of Tongues**— This one is controversial, too, but historically it has been the supernatural ability to explain what people are saying when they are speaking a language that other people in the audience don't know.
- **Helps**—This is the supernatural ability and desire to care for people and assist them in the work of God. This is similar to the gifts of service and mercy.
- **Administration**—This is related in function to the gift of leadership and is the supernatural, God-given

ability to steer, pilot, or direct the activities of churches and/or ministries in a very detailed, organized, methodical, and effective manner.

Five Key Points about Spiritual Gifts

1. "MAKING DISCIPLES" IS NOT A GIFT.

Making disciples is a command. Our spiritual gifts enable us to do a more effective job when it comes to making disciples.

2. OUR NATURAL TALENTS (OR LACK THEREOF) DO NOT NECESSARILY HAVE ANYTHING TO DO WITH OUR SPIRITUAL GIFTS.

Moses, for example, was not a natural speaker. He stuttered. But that's exactly why God gave him the supernatural ability to be a prophet, teacher, and leader, to show forth his glory through Moses' weakness.

David was the youngest member of an insignificant family of shepherds. On the face of it, he did not seem naturally suited to be a leader. But God supernaturally gifted him, and thus David became a remarkably effective Israelite leader.

The apostle Paul was naturally talented and remarkably well educated and trained as a Pharisee. But he found himself having to battle against his natural skills of speaking and persuasion in order to let God supernaturally work through him. Indeed, Paul was actually fearful of getting in the way of God's message.

Remember what Paul told the church at Corinth? "When I came to you, I did not come with eloquence or human wisdom as I proclaimed to you the testimony about God. For I resolved to know nothing while I was with you except Jesus Christ and him crucified. I came to you in weakness with great fear and trembling. My message and my preaching were not with wise and persuasive words, but with a demonstration of the Spirit's power, so that your faith might not rest on human wisdom, but on God's power" (1 Corinthians 2:1-5, NIV).

3. PAUL SAYS IT IS PERMISSIBLE TO ASK GOD TO GIVE US CERTAIN GIFTS.

In 1 Corinthians 12:31, Paul instructs disciples of the Lord Jesus to "earnestly desire the greater gifts."

In 1 Corinthians 14:1, he encourages disciples to "pursue love, yet desire earnestly spiritual gifts, but especially that you may prophesy," that they may effectively preach the Word of God and help people change their lives and follow the Lord more fully and more faithfully.

"The one who prophesies speaks to people for their strengthening, encouraging and comfort," Paul says in 1 Corinthians 14:3 (NIV), adding in verse 4 that "the one who prophesies edifies the church." Then, in verse 39, he concludes, "Therefore, my brothers and sisters, be eager to prophesy."

Paul also affirms people's desire to have the gift of leadership, the ability to lead God's people to fulfill the Great Commission.

In 1 Timothy 3:1, Paul says, "If any man aspires to the office of overseer, it is a fine work he desires to do."

Does this mean that in asking God to give us certain gifts, God is somehow obligated to say yes?

Of course not. But he might, and it is okay to ask.

4. LEADERS DON'T GIVE SPIRITUAL GIFTS. THEY DEVELOP THEM.

Help your team learn what gifts God gives.

Help them identify which gift or gifts God has individually given each of them.

Encourage them to take on projects and assignments in different kinds of ministries to help them assess what gifts they might have.

For example, give them opportunities to teach others to see if, over time, God begins using them to touch people supernaturally as they share God's truths.

Give them opportunities to serve others in the local church to see if they have a supernatural desire to meet the needs of others and seem to bless people above and beyond the call of duty when they do.

5. YOU WILL SEE SUPERNATURAL RESULTS WHEN YOU EXERCISE A SPIRITUAL GIFT.

In Ephesians 4:12-16, Paul describes the impact of disciples' employing their spiritual gifts:

- Saints are being better equipped for works of service (v. 12).
- The body of Christ is being built up (v. 12).
- The body is working together in unity (v. 13).
- Men are growing in maturity and fullness in Christ (v. 13).
- Spiritual infants are becoming spiritual adults, able to defend themselves against false teaching, and are learning to speak the truth in love as they submit to the lordship of Jesus Christ (vv. 14-16).

The Importance of the Church

God is revealing himself and his character to a lost world through his church.

Therefore, it is vital that you teach your team the role of the local church, how they fit into its structure, and how the local church fits into the structure and mission of the worldwide church.

The Four Purposes of the Church

The Bible describes the church as having four primary purposes:

1. **To show forth Christ's fullness** (Ephesians 1:22-23). Christ is the head of the church. He fills us to overflowing with himself so that through his church a lost world can see what full, abundant, invested lives look like.

2. **To show forth Christ's unity** (Ephesians 2:14-19). Christ tears down divisions. He unites us with his Father and with fellow believers so that through his church a lost world can see what love, kindness, and cooperation between genders, races, and nationalities look like.

3. **To show forth Christ's wisdom** (Ephesians 3:9-11). Christ supernaturally opens our eyes and hearts to eternal truths so that, through his church, he can help a lost world see the difference between eternal wisdom and temporal foolishness.

4. **To show forth Christ's glory** (Ephesians 3:21). Christ desires to accomplish more through his

church, through his miraculous power, than we can ask or think so that a lost world can see his might, majesty, and glory.

Every local expression of Christ's church must be faithful to these purposes and to follow the model of Acts 2:42: "They were continually devoting themselves to the apostles' teaching and to fellowship, to the breaking of bread and to prayer."

Just as Brother Bakht Singh helped plant thousands of churches according to these principles in the power of the Holy Spirit, International Assembly, the church started by the Koshys for students in Syracuse, was also established with these principles in mind.

In the book of Acts—particularly chapters 11 through 13—we find twelve biblical principles regarding the church at Antioch that are transferable to any time, place, or culture.

The Local Church in the Book of Acts

We can learn a lot about what the local church should look like by studying the book of Acts. For example:

- The local church should be global-minded, deeply committed to obeying the Great Commandments and fulfilling the Great Commission by preaching the gospel and making disciples of all nations.
- The local church should be multicultural, welcoming people of different races and ethnicities.

- The local church should have strong, mature leaders who exercise their spiritual gifts to build up the body of believers.
- The local church should have leaders of various backgrounds—racial, ethnic, and cultural.
- The local church should do everything with one accord in mind and purpose.
- The local church should be led by the Holy Spirit.
- The local church should be a worshiping church, practicing corporate worship.
- The local church should demonstrate the grace of God in practical ways.
- The local church should be a caring and compassionate church.
- The local church should send out mighty missionaries like Paul and Barnabas.
- The local church should be a praying, fasting church that continuously seeks and does the will of God.

It simply cannot be overemphasized how important it is for followers of Jesus Christ to understand the New Testament purpose, function, and organization of the church. Make sure you're equipping disciples who make the spiritual growth and depth of the local church—and the planting of new churches, particularly among unreached or under-reached people groups—their highest priority.

QUESTIONS

1. What are some issues in Scripture in which you sense the need to go deeper?

2. Evaluate yourself. Are you regularly fellowshipping with other believers? Do you tithe and give offerings on a consistent basis? Are you staying pure in heart, especially when it comes to being sexually pure?

3. Look up the following passages. What do those verses say about sexual purity? What does that mean for you?
   - Proverbs 6–7
   - Galatians 5:16
   - 2 Timothy 2:22
   - James 1:14-15; 4:1-2
   - 1 Peter 2:11
   - 1 John 2:16

4. What are two key characteristics of a good leader? How can you develop those characteristics in yourself?

5. What are your spiritual gifts?

6. What are indications to yourself and to others that these are not just natural talents but real spiritual gifts from God?

7. Are you serving the Lord using your spiritual gifts or your own strength? How can you improve in this area?

8. What are the four purposes of the church? What can you do for and in your local church to help accomplish these purposes?

TESTIMONY: LYNN A. ROSENBERG

When I was growing up on the New Jersey shore, my next-door neighbors were Christians. But my family was very involved in a Protestant church where the gospel was not shared. I did learn a few Bible stories but never how to have a personal relationship with Jesus Christ. The people there were loving and generous, yet it was more like a social club than a church.

My Christian neighbors held a children's Bible club the summer I was eight years old, and they invited all the kids in the neighborhood. It was there that I heard the whole gospel, and I asked for God's forgiveness and began my spiritual life in Christ.

My neighbors moved away a few years later, but the Lord kept in my heart the lingering longing to know more of him.

I can look back and see the Lord's many ways of protecting me over the years as I grew through grade school and high school. In my senior year I auditioned for the drama department of Syracuse University and was accepted to begin in August 1986. The Lord took me to Syracuse, New York, where I would finally be welcomed into a community of believers.

Debbi DeCola was on the staff of Campus Crusade for Christ, a student ministry at S.U. I went to an ice cream party that Crusade sponsored and met Debbi, who made an appointment with me to talk one-on-one about the Lord. She shared the gospel with me, and I shared my story with her. "I'm a Christian, but what do I do next?" I said. I was like a baby. I knew I was alive. I knew I was helpless. I knew who my Father was. But I didn't know much else—*and I was very hungry*.

Debbi was wonderful. She began to meet with me each week and invited me to be a part of a small group of other young Christian women. She taught me how to pray and how to study the Bible for myself. We went on evangelism appointments together, and I learned to share my faith by watching her lovingly interact with students who were searching for the truth. Debbi invited me to prayer meetings and to retreats and game nights. She gave me what I needed the most as a young believer—she loved me and she fed me, literally and spiritually.

Often I would find myself at her home having dinner with her and her husband, Nick. To this day I make some of the recipes I learned from her—poppy seed chicken and chicken puffs are two of them. I remember her dinner plates; they had little farm scenes on them. I wanted to have plates just like hers one day. When she found out I had never heard of the Anne of Green Gables novels and movies, she exclaimed, "But you're Anne! We're having a sleepover movie marathon tonight!"

She also told me the story of how she and Nick met and courted and married. I wanted to have the same kind of love story myself. I saw how she and Nick ministered together on the campus with students, how their marriage was a real partnership and team, how they prayed faithfully for their own children.

Their first son was born in August when I was home for the summer. When she was expecting their twins a few years later, Debbi had a difficult time physically and was on bed rest for a long time. I remember feeling so helpless, wanting to help her. She said, "What would really help is if you'd sit here and cry with me." I could do that! And so I learned to "weep with those who weep" (Romans 12:15). I was with friends in the waiting room of the hospital when their twins were eventually born.

With the birth of her children, Debbi "changed jobs," and her time on campus decreased for a season. But Debbi was still my friend and "spiritual mom," and we have continued that friendship to this day.

After my first year at Syracuse University, I committed my life to full-time service for the Lord. I thought maybe I'd be involved in a drama ministry or go overseas as a missionary after graduation. As I prayed and worked to that end, the Lord began to burden my heart for the international students on campus. Through friendships and the courtship of Joel Rosenberg—now my husband—I was introduced to the Koshys.

I will always remember the first time I attended International Assembly, where Dr. Koshy is the pastor. There I saw people from all around the world, people with Indian saris and colorful African dresses, people praising the Lord on their knees in Urdu and Chinese and various Indian dialects and with beautifully accented English. I was in heaven.

The first Sunday I attended, I was warmly greeted by Dr. Koshy and his wife and invited to their home for lunch after the service. It was a cold, dreary Syracuse winter day, but as I entered their home, it was like the cold and loneliness of the day melted away.

Their living room was full of vibrant colors, Oriental carpets and round gold pillows, shiny brass vases and carved wooden elephants. There were people gathered around the kitchen counters, helping Mrs. Koshy finish the preparation of fragrant yellow rice, thick curried chicken, spicy sauces, and battered vegetables. And there was warm chapati—soft, round, flat skillet bread. The colors and scents alone were a feast. Mrs. Koshy hugged me warmly, introduced me to many people, and asked me to assist in preparing the salad. As I stood there peeling cucumbers, I looked around at the kind faces and listened to their discussion of the day's sermon and sighed with contentment.

I spent many afternoons at the Koshys' house. I joined their prayer meetings held in an old, cozy farmhouse the church owned, perched on a hill overlooking Syracuse. I began to teach a Chinese student conversational English. I attended the international lunches held each week on campus, with free food and a guest speaker (almost always a believer who would share a testimony about how he or she came to know Christ personally)—the place to meet international students and begin wonderful friendships.

As I became a part of the ministry, I was continually blessed and humbled by the fervency of the Koshys' love for Christ and love for people. They taught me to never love "the ministry" or "the work" but to truly love the Lord and his dear ones whom he brings into our lives. I'll never tire of Mrs. Koshy's hugs and "Come, dear."

The Koshys began to meet with a small group of American students every weekday at 7 a.m. for further discipleship. Dr. Koshy invited Joel and me to be a part of this group, and so we began to have an even deeper understanding of the Koshys' hearts and the ministry God had given them. They took us in the Scriptures every morning, studying Ephesians and various other books of the Bible. They taught us about biblical worship and about the purpose of the church. We took copious notes on how to live as disciples of Christ, how to have an intense prayer life, how to abide in Christ, and about the ministry of hospitality. We heard the amazing stories of their years walking with Jesus and many of the adventures he'd taken them on. He is the Provider of all we need and more than we could ask, dream, or imagine!

Some mornings Dr. Koshy would use Joel and me as an example and teach on the relationship of Christ and the church (bridegroom and bride) or on the importance of prayer ("What if Joel and Lynn never spoke to each other?"). I would blush but love the fact that Koshy really knew us and cared for us.

The Koshys gave us assignments—passing out invitations to an international student picnic, hosting prayer times for the Billy Graham crusade that was coming to town (and would be held in the Carrier Dome on our campus), serving food at the international friendship lunches, taking new believers under our wings, giving our testimonies at church. They believed in us, trusted us, counseled us, and laughed with us. They cared for us like their own children.

One winter I came down with mononucleosis. I slept through an exam. I could barely move. I managed to make it down to the student health clinic, where Mrs. (Dr.) Koshy was a campus physician. She took a look at me, prayed with me, and announced that I must come and stay with them until I recovered. I don't even remember how I got to their house, but soon I was snuggled under blankets in their guest room and they were bringing me carafes of cool water and hot homemade chicken soup.

When I was starting to feel a bit better, I was allowed to come upstairs, and they wrapped me up in blankets and sat me in a reclining chair by the window. I remember looking out into their backyard and watching the snow steadily falling and crying with joy that I was so loved.

Joel and I married in the summer of 1990, only a few weeks after my graduation from Syracuse University. Dr. Koshy officiated. We moved to the city of Washington, D.C.—a beautiful and powerful place. People say that after only a short time of living in D.C., one can catch "Potomac fever"—a great and unshakable love for this city of marble and cherry blossoms, crisscrossed by the Potomac River. It's true.

Joel and I were led to join a growing evangelical church

in the northern Virginia suburbs. But we were not pre-pared for the difficult transition from ministry on a college campus to ministry in "real life." We came with big dreams for ministry, which always turned out to be too extrava-gant and far-reaching. Additionally crippled by a definite lack of administrative skills, we failed many times in vari-ous ministries. We made plans to start a church-wide prayer ministry for missions. We created a course on evangelism for the church body. We taught in our young marrieds Sunday school class. We led follow-up teams for evangelistic events. We taught the two-year-old Sunday school kids. We spent a lot of time and energy considering an opportunity to lead our adult Sunday school class in some bold new visions of ministry. And in the process we got very tired and were con-sistently unsatisfied.

Then one of our pastors asked us to quietly begin a min-istry of personal discipleship. His hope was for the vision of discipleship to "bubble up" from within the church instead of the top-down approaches he had tried that had been ineffective. So in 1997 we went back to Syracuse for a visit. We stayed with the Koshys in their warm, memory-filled home. We spent time with the DeColas, also.

To both families we posed the same questions: What should we do to serve the Lord in Washington? How do we lead people to focus on the basics of ministry—evangelism, discipleship, and missions? How could we begin a disciple-ship ministry?

Dr. Koshy told us that the first thing to do was gather some people together for prayer. That would be the begin-ning of any work of the Lord. The Koshys and the DeColas reminded us of what we'd been taught, of what we'd experienced in Syracuse.

We drove home from that trip filled with excitement about putting our "heritage" into use—combining warm hospitality with purposeful evangelism and discipleship. We began with prayer. At first, only Joel, my mom, and I were there to pray. But as we began to pray, the Lord began to unfold his plans for us.

The phone rang one day, and it was this pastor at our church encouraging Joel to call a young man named John Black, a new believer who wanted help in getting started in his relationship with the Lord. John became a true treasure in our lives. He truly was "F.A.T."—faithful, available, and teachable. He asked us a million questions and began applying the Word of God in every area of his life.

Next, my sister Susan—a new believer—asked me to disciple her. Then her friend Kailea wanted to be discipled. These two bright, energetic, beautiful women kept me on my toes, also asking so many questions and faithfully applying to their own lives what I was teaching them from the Scriptures. And it kept building from there. Soon, Joel was leading a discipleship team of five men and I was leading a discipleship team of six women. God has done an amazing work in their lives, not because of our great wisdom (ha!) or insight, but because of God's blessing on the simple obedience of investing time, love, and God's truth into the lives of other believers. Most began as spiritual children, but they grew rapidly in grace and maturity. All of them emerged as young leaders in our church—most eventually joined the staff of our church—hungry to serve the Lord and passionately committed to those they shepherd and disciple.

The women came over to our home for a meal, prayer, and Bible study time every other week. Part of my goal was to envelop them in the warmth and comfort of home and hearth. I wanted to give them an oasis from our busy and driven city. My other goal was to challenge them to more fully live the Great Commandments (to love the Lord with all your heart, and your neighbor as yourself) and the Great Commission (to go and make disciples).

With all the opportunities and needs competing for their time, with all the temptations of youth surrounding them, our prayer was to help them love and serve God and others with excellence, endurance, and a cheerful heart. It was a dream come true to work with these men and women.

In the years since, I have always sought out women to invest in spiritually. The Lord has blessed me with a wide variety of opportunities, including meeting with single moms, married couples (alongside my husband), and international people. In 2006, the Lord led Joel and me to begin a nonprofit organization, The Joshua Fund, with the goal to mobilize Christians to "bless Israel and her neighbors in the name of Jesus, according to Genesis 12:1-3" (to learn more, go to www.joshuafund.net). Many of those first disciples have traveled to the Middle East with us, served on our board, and even worked for Joel full-time for a season. They have become co-laborers and kindred spirits.

Over the years, I was delighted to be invited to teach at various women's conferences, classes, and gatherings about what God had taught me regarding our biblical mandate to make disciples of all nations. In the process, I met a dear friend named Dixie who had the same vision. The director of women's ministry at our church met with Dixie and me several times and encouraged us to prayerfully set a goal of "making discipleship part of the culture among the women of our church." It was a bit audacious, but we felt the Holy Spirit nudging us to say yes.

We met together and prayed, "Lord, show us how to do this!" Soon we started by finding two other mature, godly women who had experience in disciple making. We asked them to join us as leaders so that we could start this ministry with four quartets, four little groups of disciples that each of the four of us would be leading. Then we approached several pastors and ministry leaders in the church and asked them to recommend women they knew who were rising leaders and could be disciple makers but needed some initial encouragement and training. Our hope in this phase was not to find new believers or young believers to disciple but to find women who were already mature in their faith but lacked either the vision, a tool, or a model to disciple others. Our goal, in short, was to prayerfully recruit and train trainers, women who could turn around in fairly short order and begin taking new and young believers under their wings and begin investing heavily in them. We wanted to create a community of like-minded women who could encourage each other, hold each other accountable to fulfilling the Great Commission, and then actually begin multiplying their impact.

The Lord provided thirteen women that first year. We divided them into groups of three, assigned each a leader, and established a common schedule. We would meet every other week as small groups in the homes of the quartet leaders, and on the other weeks we would meet all together as a large group. While we wanted to draw on the principles of *The Invested Life* to give these women the big picture concerning discipleship, we were also looking for some curriculum that would help us take these women through the basics of the faith in a systematic way that they could easily replicate and take younger believers through. Dixie had studied at the C. S. Lewis Institute here in northern Virginia and had been introduced to a book called *Discipleship Essentials* by a pastor named Greg Ogden. The book covered the basics of the Christian faith in a thorough and serious way, though we made a few tweaks to make it line up fully with our church's doctrinal position. The more we considered the book, the more excited we became. We had found our tool!

Our group began in the fall and went through the school year. We spent two weeks on each chapter (or grouping of chapters sometimes), one week discussing it with the large group and one week going more in depth with the small group. But we didn't just take these women through the study. We did our best to make the process more personal and more practical. We attended church conferences together, served at homeless shelters, hosted neighborhood outreaches, served as prayer counselors at church ministry events, took a Saturday in the country as a mini retreat together, and enjoyed holiday parties and mission gatherings together. At the end of the school year, Dixie and I "commissioned" the thirteen women to "go and make disciples" wherever the Lord led them. We stayed in touch and created a quarterly gathering to share a meal, encourage one another, and hear how the Lord was working in each of their lives.

When we were ready to start up for the next year, we had thirty-two new women involved. We created two branches of sixteen women each. As we entered our third year, we spread to multiple congregations, with each branch running with its own schedule, style, and leadership. Dixie and I prayed and decided that for our two branches, we'd extend the time together from one school year (about nine months) to eighteen months before "commissioning" the women to disciple others. This enabled the groups to go through the material a bit slower, spend much more time on personal application and accountability, and do more ministry projects together. All the various leaders from the different branches would get together once a month to address questions, pray for one another, and dream about the future. What a joy it was to see the number of women investing in other women growing more and more! Bit by bit, we hope and pray for even more women to be able to answer those two simple questions with joy: "Who is investing in me?" and "Whom am I investing in?"

After some initial years of tiring ourselves out as we tried a number of ministries we weren't really called to or gifted for, Joel and I can truly say with the apostle Paul, "Now we really live" (1 Thessalonians 3:8) because of the ministry of discipleship to which the Lord has called us. Our lives have certainly changed quite a bit along the way. Today, we have four sons, Caleb, Jacob, Jonah, and Noah. My husband has transitioned from an all-consuming political career to life as an author, speaker, and ministry leader. And I have been homeschooling all my boys since Caleb was in third grade. People ask me how I can possibly fit everything in, how I can do all of this. Believe me, I'm no superhero! But I know that I can do all things through Christ, who strengthens me, just as the Scriptures teach.

Walking by faith takes what some would call "reckless optimism." Trust me, it's the only way to really live! When our sons were little and we were first getting started with discipleship in the Washington area, the boys and I used to play the "pick up" game. We would run around the main part of the house, throwing any clutter into a bin and stashing it in the laundry room to get our home looking half-decent. Then we'd pray together before the discipleship groups would arrive. I'd tell the boys, "These wonderful folks need your hugs and a big, big welcome when they arrive!" We would dim the lights and light a candle—everything looked better! Our culture teaches that your house needs to be perfect before you can host people. It's not true!

The Bible commands *all* believers to "practice hospitality," so don't think it's not your cup of tea. The Bible doesn't say to perfect hospitality, but to practice it! Your job is to welcome and love, and we can all do that.

Galatians 2:20 says, "It is no longer I who live, but Christ lives in me." Learning to walk in the power of the Holy Spirit, enjoying the sweetness of fellowship with the Lord, keeping the priorities of evangelism and discipleship in sight, and beginning your day with a willing spirit—these are the keys to being able to respond with an obedient heart. And God blesses obedience! Through obedience we abide closely with Christ and therefore we bear fruit. Isn't that what we read in John 15?

The Lord has also provided for us in ways that are amazing. He brought along my mom to help us, and what a huge help she has been. In fact, she was our first discipleship prayer partner. We have been so fortunate that she lives locally, moving here around the time Caleb was a baby. She loves to interact with all these young disciples, she helps me so much with hospitality, and she loves our boys and loves to have them over to her home. Several years ago, my sister and another dear friend and I began to homeschool together and share each other's burdens and joys. That has not only been a fruit of discipleship but has made discipleship more possible in our lives. Other women in the discipleship groups have also brought their gifts of service and administration to fill in for our many weaknesses. The point is, as we have sought to be faithful in obeying the Great Commission, the Lord has provided in real and practical and often unexpected ways to help us serve him. And all the while our sons have had the chance to see what it looks like when Dad and Mom make the Great Commission a real family priority. Personally, I can't think of a better gift to our boys than to be a part of loving these disciples of Jesus Christ with us. Seeing our family as a team—with the mission to love and reach the world in the name of Jesus Christ—is the way we always dreamed life would be.

Through my time in Syracuse I was blessed with real saints of the Lord who discipled me. Their days were filled with teaching me God's Word, correcting my youthful foolishness, loving me deeply, and showing me how life should be lived. I will always strive to model what I learned from the DeColas and the Koshys—that life is only abundant and meaningful and full of joy when it is lived for the Lord and for others, when it is invested with the intent of seeing lives saved and completed in Christ.

———

All that said, I also wanted to share with you the testimony of one of the women with whom I've been blessed to walk this journey. I hope you find it helpful as you consider how you too can invest in someone's life.

My Experience with *The Invested Life*
By Kailea Hunt

Discipleship used to be a very scary and intimidating word to me. I still remember the conversation I had with Joel about discipleship over a decade ago. Little did I realize it would change my life and future ministry forever.

I was at Joel and Lynn's home to assist in hosting a lunch for newcomers to our church. After almost everyone had left the luncheon, Joel started asking me about my life story. He soon got the impression I was a pretty mature believer. Raised in a Christian home, I first accepted Jesus as my Lord and Savior at the age of nine at a Christian summer camp. My experience growing up in the church included two services on Sunday, Wednesday night youth group, and participating in every summer camp and youth group function possible. I even attended a Christian liberal arts college nearby.

However, through all those years spent in the church, I was neither discipled one-on-one nor taught how to disciple others. The only time the topic of making disciples really entered my purview was in sermons and lessons on evangelism and missions using the Great Commission in Matthew 28:19-20.

So when Joel asked me if I was interested in discipling others, I completely freaked out (both on the inside and out)! There was no way I was prepared to disciple others. I didn't even know what that meant or how to do it. Later, Lynn told me that she scolded Joel for asking me about discipleship because she already knew that I was afraid of the topic and felt very inadequate!

Still, I noticed that Lynn was beginning to disciple her sister Susan. I could see Susan growing rapidly in her faith, and I wanted to grow more too. Before long, I asked Lynn if I could join her time with Susan, and fortunately she said yes. As we began to share our lives with one another, discipleship soon became the biggest blessing to my spiritual walk.

I can't adequately begin to explain how being discipled made an impact in my life, but I'm going to try. Joel and Lynn—but Lynn more specifically—poured out their lives and their love to me as an overflow of their walk with Christ. Lynn and I began to meet one-on-one and also with Susan and then with more women as they too eventually joined the group. Through our times together, we shared our testimonies, our dreams, our fears, and relationship highs and lows. We studied the Bible, we prayed, we fellowshipped, we shared meals, we spent times in worship, and we even participated in international mission trips together. We spent vacations and holidays together. We shared in the joys of marriages, births of new children, and even mourned the loss of close loved ones. In short, we did life together, and it was what I needed.

While I continued soaking in all I could from a personal perspective in this discipleship relationship, the Lord called me into full-time vocational ministry at our church. I served with Global Impact, our short-term mission trip ministry. And as the pastor and I began to focus on developing our leaders, the Lord burdened our hearts to weave discipleship throughout the ministry. We had leadership retreats where guest speakers (Joel and Lynn being some of them) focused on the topic of discipleship. We used an early version of *The Invested Life* manuscript as a tool and resource for our leaders. We consistently kept the topic of discipleship at the forefront of everyone's mind. Soon it became a natural piece of what our ministry was about as we implemented it from the top down. Staff poured into coordinators, coordinators poured into coaches, coaches poured into leaders, and leaders poured into team members. I will be the first to admit it wasn't always perfect in implementation. However, our desire was that it be a key ingredient to a successful ministry model, and I believe it was the impetus for the ministry to be efficiently volunteer driven.

There have been many lessons I've learned about discipleship from not only experiencing it firsthand but also studying it. One key thing I learned that helped alleviate some anxiety was that I could do it right where I was at. I realized I needed to be a good steward with those the Lord had entrusted to me in my own sphere of influence. So as I served in Global Impact, I pursued women who were already young leaders in the ministry to disciple. This allowed me to be very efficient and focused with my time and energy, as opposed to trying to disciple people in a different ministry from the one I was already committed to.

Now I serve in a different role at our church. But I continue to pursue discipleship relationships as the Lord brings them to me. Some women seek me out and ask me to prayerfully consider discipling them. Other women I have sought out on my own because of their "F.A.T.-ness" (faithful, available, teachable).

Discipleship, I've learned, is about being intentional. As I look back over the early years of my life, I see the Lord's provision of specific people in each stage of life who poured into me, challenged me, and encouraged my walk with the Lord. But until I moved to the Washington, D.C., area, none of them intentionally pursued me and equipped me to go and do likewise. Lynn and Joel, however, were intentional in their pursuit of me, and they encouraged me to pursue others and seek to invest in the lives of others. The two main questions they taught me to ask myself have been the same two questions I've been able to challenge others around me with: "Who is investing in you?" and "Whom are you investing in?"

Intentionality also plays into the purpose of the relationship. In the first few discipleship relationships I attempted, I did not do a great job of instilling a deep understanding of and desire to reproduce the model. But more recently I believe I've been able to improve and focus more on the purpose and value of discipleship so others feel more equipped to replicate it.

Obviously discipleship is meant to be gender specific. You can be challenged and grow in your walk by the life and leadership of men and women all around you. But true, healthy, fruitful one-on-one discipleship must occur in the safety of same-gender relationships.

I've learned that discipleship relationships differ in their lengths. Although I've latched on to the Rosenberg family and feel like I'm "one of the family"—mostly because I don't ever want to let go of their friendship and role in my life—this doesn't always occur with every relationship. There are some relationships that are unique and special and last a lifetime. But there are some that are meant to be for a season. Neither is right or wrong. But it's always wise to keep a healthy perspective and be self-aware and discerning in each discipleship relationship.

I've had my share of "casualties" over the years. Some women I pursued might have initially seemed "F.A.T." But over the course of weeks, months, or even a year, they proved that they weren't. I've had difficult relationships where the chemistry or the character just wasn't there. And some of the casualties have been my fault due to my own personal issues. But God continues to show me how to stay the course and not give up hope. He redeems all things and allows us to grow from our experiences.

Being discipled has been the most powerful tool the Lord has used in my life to make me the person I am today—as a wife, mother, friend, and co-laborer. On a personal note, it has shown me what unconditional love can look like on earth. It's given me the opportunity to heal from past wounds and heartache and shown me how to minister more effectively to others through those past experiences. I cannot imagine my life without it. Discipleship has spurred me on in my love for the Lord, his Word, and his work.

Since meeting Lynn and Joel, I've learned a lot about discipleship. The first of many lessons is that it's easier than you think. Any maturing follower of Christ can do it and should. Making disciples is a command from Christ. There's no option other than to ignore it and be disobedient. You don't have to be an expert in theology, have a seminary degree, or be really old to offer something to someone. No matter where you are in your relationship with Christ or how long you've been walking faithfully with him, there is always someone who can learn from you. And there always will be until the Lord calls us home.

CHAPTER EIGHT

WORSHIP TOGETHER

*You shall fear only the LORD your God; and you
shall worship Him.*

DEUTERONOMY 6:13

As human beings—and certainly as true disciples of the Lord
Jesus Christ—we were created to worship the King of kings
and the Lord of lords. Unfortunately, worship is too often
misunderstood and overlooked as part of the Christian life.
So let us invest some time learning a few deeper truths about
this vital topic. And let us be intentional about worshiping
together.

We were not simply created to *thank* God for the great
things he has done for us, nor simply to *ask* him to do more
great things for us, even things such as helping us lead people
to Christ and make disciples of all nations. No, we were created to worship the Lord our God for *who he is.* Thus, we
must be intentional about slowing down, retreating from the
world, and entering the Lord's presence to truly worship the
God who loves us and gave himself for us.

In Revelation 7:9-12, we see a beautiful vision of heaven:

> I looked, and behold, a great multitude which no
> one could count, from every nation and all tribes
> and peoples and tongues, standing before the throne
> and before the Lamb, clothed in white robes, and
> palm branches were in their hands; and they cry out
> with a loud voice, saying, "Salvation to our God who
> sits on the throne, and to the Lamb." And all the
> angels were standing around the throne and around
> the elders and the four living creatures; and they fell
> on their faces before the throne and worshiped God,
> saying, "Amen, blessing and glory and wisdom and
> thanksgiving and honor and power and might, be to
> our God forever and ever. Amen."

Scripture teaches us that God wants a people redeemed
by the precious blood of the Lord Jesus Christ out of every
nation, tribe, people, and language group worshiping the
King in the beauty of his holiness.

What, then, is your ultimate destination and mine?

To be in heaven, worshiping the King of kings and the
Lord of lords. Alone? Not at all. The Scriptures teach us
that we will be worshiping God with disciples from every
nation. In eternity, we are going to have the opportunity to
truly worship the Lord and give him the praise of which he
alone is worthy and which we owe him since he saved us and
redeemed our sinful, wretched lives when he didn't have to.

The first time worship is mentioned in Scripture is when
Abraham took Isaac up Mount Moriah and told his servants,

"We will worship and then we will come back to you" (Genesis 22:5, NIV). What was Abraham taking to offer to God? His very best, his miraculous firstborn son, Isaac. How precious, then, that thousands of years later, God the Father—the God of Abraham, Isaac, and Jacob—sacrificed his very best, his only begotten Son, Jesus Christ, on that very same mountain.

Worship is costly. It requires giving God our very best. That's why when David went to worship one day and a man named Araunah offered to give David for free anything he needed to make a sacrifice to the Lord, David insisted upon paying. "I will not sacrifice to the LORD my God burnt offerings that cost me nothing," said David, the man after God's own heart (2 Samuel 24:24, NIV).

In worship, we come to give, not to receive. We come to minister to the Lord, just as the wise men traveled a long distance at their own expense to give costly gifts to the baby Jesus, not expecting anything in return (Matthew 2:11).

Consider the following verses:

- "My sons, do not be negligent now, for the LORD has chosen you to stand before Him, to minister to Him, and to be His ministers and burn incense" (2 Chronicles 29:11).
- "Worship the LORD with reverence and rejoice with trembling" (Psalm 2:11).
- "Shout joyfully to God, all the earth; sing the glory of His name; make His praise glorious. Say to God, 'How awesome are Your works! Because of the greatness of Your power Your enemies will give feigned obedience to You. All the earth will worship You, and

will sing praises to You; they will sing praises to Your name" (Psalm 66:1-4).

- "Come, let us worship and bow down, let us kneel before the LORD our Maker. For He is our God, and we are the people of His pasture and the sheep of His hand" (Psalm 95:6-7).
- "Give to the LORD, O families of the peoples, give to the LORD glory and strength. Give to the LORD the glory due His name; bring an offering, and come into His courts. Oh, worship the LORD in the beauty of holiness! Tremble before Him, all the earth" (Psalm 96:7-9, NKJV).
- "An hour is coming, and now is, when the true worshipers will worship the Father in spirit and truth; for such people the Father seeks to be His worshipers. God is spirit, and those who worship Him must worship in spirit and truth" (John 4:23-24).

Just imagine: God has chosen you and me to worship him. What an awesome honor and privilege that the God of the universe desires our worship, which alone can satisfy his heart.

In fact, Scripture teaches us that true disciples are to

- worship the Lord by ministering to him—to focus completely on praising him and pleasing him, not thinking about ourselves;
- worship the Lord by giving to him—by bringing him our time, our talents, and our treasure;
- worship the Lord corporately—in a great multitude;

- worship the Lord cross-culturally—with people from every nation;
- worship the Lord by bowing down before him— honoring him upon our knees as the King of kings;
- worship the Lord in reverence and with trembling— with great respect and awe;
- worship the Lord joyfully—not depressed or gloomy;
- worship the Lord with singing—regardless of how well we sing;
- worship the Lord in spirit—that is, as believers, born again and filled with the Holy Spirit of God; and
- worship the Lord in truth—being careful to be true to the Word of God and not veering off with our own ideas or our own concept of God.

Worshiping in Spirit and Truth

Are you asking, "How exactly should I worship? What specifically do I do?" Those are good questions, for you and those in whose lives you're investing.

The Lord has asked two things of us when we worship him. The first, as already mentioned, is that we worship him "in spirit and truth" (John 4:21-24). The second is that we partake of the Lord's Table, also commonly known as Communion (1 Corinthians 11:23-26). Let me explain.

To worship "in spirit" means we must enter worship in the power of the Holy Spirit. Thus, you must confess your sins, repent and turn back to the Lord, and ask him to fill you to overflowing with his Holy Spirit.

It is essential that you prepare for worship in purity and

enter with the mind-set that you are there to minister to the Lord—to please him, not yourself—by giving yourself to him as a living sacrifice. Therefore, you need to clear your heart of the stains of sin and clear your mind of the distractions of life. Rid your thinking of life's "to do" lists. Be disciplined not to ask God for anything at this point. That can come later. But be careful not to think about the things that you want and need and wish for. That causes you to focus on yourself, not on the Lord. Focus wholly and completely on the greatness of our great God—on his holiness, his beauty, his majesty, his power, his sacrificial love, and on the great things he has done for his people throughout history. Come into his presence because you are in love with him, and shower him with praise for who he is.

Here are some practical suggestions for clearing your mind and focusing on God:

- Gather together with other believers, or hide yourself away where it is quiet and private.
- Kneel down before the Lord in an attitude of humility and reverence.
- Close your eyes to eliminate the distractions around you.
- Listen to praise music that exalts the name of Jesus and reminds you that the joy of the Lord is your strength.
- Sing praise songs to the Lord.
- Sing classic hymns to the Lord.
- Sing children's worship songs to the Lord—sometimes their very simplicity will help you focus on the simple, eternal, fundamental truths of God's greatness and glory.

- Play an instrument in worship to the Lord.
- Read the Psalms out loud to the Lord.
- Repeat Scriptures that you've memorized.
- Audibly express your praises to the Lord, if you'd like.
- Lift up your hands to the Lord, if you'd like.

Such acts prepare our hearts for true worship. They clear our minds and focus our attention on the One who is so worthy of our praise and adoration.

We must also realize that whether the Lord has given us a lot or a little—whether we feel blessed by him at the moment or we somehow feel deprived by him—we must still enter his presence and praise him for who he is, because he deserves our praise.

Now here's a critical point: praise is different from thanksgiving.

We *thank* God for what he has done for us specifically. But we *praise* him for who he is, regardless of our circumstances. Let us explain why.

Let's say you are in church thanking the Lord out loud for your new job, the health of your children, and all your material blessings. But the person sitting or kneeling next to you has just lost his job, his children are very ill, and he has very few if any material blessings. What if you were in church next to Job? How would it help him draw nearer to the Lord to hear you thanking the Lord for his unique blessings on you? It would be far better for you both to *praise* the Lord for who he is, regardless of your circumstances, because this lifts your eyes to his greatness and power and eternal love and away from yourselves. If you are going to thank the

Lord publicly during worship, then thank him for what Jesus Christ has done for all mankind to keep your focus upon his death, burial, and resurrection. This will be a blessing to you and to those around you.

Think of the words of the prophet Habakkuk when he wrote, "Though the fig tree does not bud and there are no grapes on the vines, though the olive crop fails and the fields produce no food, though there are no sheep in the pen and no cattle in the stalls, yet I will rejoice in the LORD, I will be joyful in God my Savior. The Sovereign LORD is my strength; he makes my feet like the feet of a deer, he enables me to tread on the heights" (Habakkuk 3:17-19, NIV).

How is that possible? How can we worship when life looks bleak?

This is what is meant by worshiping the Lord "in truth"— getting our thoughts off our present circumstances and remembering Christ, who is "the Truth" (John 14:6), and on his eternal precepts, which are rock solid and can never be shaken or changed.

Now that you are ready to enter true worship, invest long periods of time gratefully acknowledging these eternal, enduring truths:

- Our God is the one true and living God.
- Our God is all-powerful.
- Our God is all-knowing.
- Our God is all-caring.
- Our God is all-loving.
- Our God made the heavens and the earth.
- Our God made the stars above and the seas below.

- Our God made the beasts of the field and the birds of the air.
- Our God made men and women in his image.
- Our God sent the Lord Jesus Christ to live on this earth and die and rise again for us.
- Our God saved us and called us to a holy life, not because of anything we have done but because of his own purpose and grace.
- Our God loves us with an everlasting love.
- Our God gave us his holy Word.
- Our God sent us his Holy Spirit to teach us, convict us, and comfort and guide us.
- Our God established the church as his body, of which the Lord Jesus is the head.
- Our God allows us by his grace to enter his house with thanksgiving and his courts with praise.

One way to worship is to spend time meditating on the names of God as found in the Bible. We learn a lot about God's character through the various names he gives himself:

- **Elohim** ("God")—Genesis 1:1
- **El Elyon** ("Most High God")—Genesis 14:18
- **Adonai** ("Lord")—Genesis 15:2
- **El Shaddai** ("Almighty God")—Genesis 17:1
- **El Olam** ("Everlasting God")—Genesis 21:33
- **El Elohe Israel** ("God, the God of Israel")— Genesis 33:20
- **El Gibbor** ("Mighty God")—Isaiah 9:6, 7
- **Jehovah-Jireh** ("God my provider")—Genesis 22:14

- **Jehovah-Rapha** ("God my healer")—Exodus 15:26
- **Jehovah-Nissi** ("God my banner")—Exodus 17:15
- **Jehovah-M'Kaddesh** ("God who sanctifies")—Leviticus 20:8
- **Jehovah-Shalom** ("God of peace")—Judges 6:24
- **Jehovah-Sabaoth** ("God of hosts")—1 Samuel 17:45
- **Jehovah-Elyon** ("Most High God")—Psalm 7:17
- **Jehovah-Roi** ("God my shepherd")—Psalm 23:1
- **Jehovah-Tsidkenui** ("God our righteousness")—Jeremiah 23:6
- **Jehovah-Shammah** ("God is there")—Ezekiel 48:35

Many churches hold "worship" services that really don't involve true worship. They read Scriptures. They sing. They listen to the choir. Then the pastor preaches. This is all wonderful. But it's actually a praise and teaching service, not a worship service.

Again, singing is just the beginning. According to the Scriptures, actual worship literally means *bowing down* before the Lord and ministering to him, giving to him, acknowledging his worth, and praising him for who he is. This is the part of worship that many churches, unfortunately, never get to. Yet this is where we are focused on him, not us. This is where we please the Lord, where we make him happy by appreciating him, spending time with him, and experiencing sweet fellowship with him.

At International Assembly, we begin with about ten to fifteen minutes of singing and Bible reading and some short encouragement from God's Word. But then the entire congregation—including the children—sets apart time for corporate worship. People literally get down on their knees and talk to the Lord, silently or audibly, one after the other. Some feel moved to lead the congregation in singing a praise song or some verses of a hymn everyone knows. Others read Scriptures of praise and adoration to the Lord, perhaps a psalm, Hannah's song (1 Samuel 2:1-10), Mary's song (Luke 1:46-55), Zacharias's prophecy (Luke 1:67-79), or the songs of the angels and elders (Revelation 4:8-11). Those from other countries are encouraged to worship in their native languages.

As we are on our knees worshiping the Lord and lifting up his name, some find themselves unable to articulate how much they love the Lord, and they remain silent. Some find themselves welling up with emotion, and they cry softly. People are respectful of one another. We are careful to maintain a sense of dignity and honor. But the important thing is that we give everyone the time to be in the presence of the Lord himself.

This takes some getting used to, we realize, for those who have little or no experience actually worshiping the Lord the way the Bible describes worship. Many pastors have never experienced true worship. Indeed, many pastors feel there isn't enough time in their services for such worship.

But we ask you: if we don't teach people what true worship is, or if we deny them some time to come into the presence of the Lord, to bow before him, to praise and adore him, are we not cheating God of the glory that is due him?

What pleasure does God get from us if we only sit in the pews and listen to a choir or watch a slide show or see a video or listen to a sermon?

Properly done, those can all be good things. But those are ways of ministering to us, the body of Christ. Worship is about ministering to the Lord himself, and we dare not deny him that which pleases him.

The Lord's Table

Another vital aspect of worship is the Lord's Table, also known as Communion.

The Lord's Table is the superlative aspect of the believer's worship. In other words, partaking of Communion is the greatest thing that we can do for the Lord Jesus Christ in obedience to his desire. For he said, "Do this in remembrance of Me" (Luke 22:19).

In 1 Corinthians 11:23-26, the apostle Paul described the sacrament of Communion this way:

> For I received from the Lord that which I also
> delivered to you, that the Lord Jesus in the night in
> which He was betrayed took bread; and when He
> had given thanks, He broke it and said, "This is
> My body, which is for you; do this in remembrance
> of Me." In the same way He took the cup also
> after supper, saying, "This cup is the new covenant
> in My blood; do this, as often as you drink it, in
> remembrance of Me." For as often as you eat this
> bread and drink the cup, you proclaim the Lord's
> death until He comes.

We read in Acts 2:42 that the early disciples gathered together for the "breaking of bread," which refers to Communion. We also read in Acts 20:7 that "on the first day of the week . . . [the disciples] were gathered together to break bread." While Jesus didn't mandate how often we should take Communion, we do see from these verses the model that the first disciples followed, that is, taking Communion every week.

So at International Assembly we take Communion every week, just after every man, woman, and child of us has had time to hear some Scriptures, sing some songs, and then spend some real time on our knees before our Maker and Redeemer. Now our hearts are ready. Now we are truly remembering what the Lord has done for each one of us. Now we are no longer distracted by the worries of the world and the duties of our daily lives. Now we are ready to eat the bread and drink the cup and celebrate the death and resurrection and the return of the Lord Jesus Christ.

We also learn through the Lord's Table the oneness and unity of the body of Christ, which is the church.

In 1 Corinthians 10:16-17, Paul writes, "Is not the cup of thanksgiving for which we give thanks a participation in the blood of Christ? And is not the bread that we break a participation in the body of Christ? Because there is one loaf, we, who are many, are one body, for we all share the one loaf" (NIV).

When we are one in spirit as the body of believers, we find it inspires us to serve those without Christ with more passion, more boldness, and more effectiveness than when we feel lonely and disconnected.

The Posture of Worship

When the president of the United States enters a room, everyone stands. In other countries, when a king or queen enters the room, everyone bows down or falls prostrate. These are signs of respect, signs of reverence.

Did you know that the Hebrew word for *worship* in the Old Testament—*shachah*—means "to bow down"? Did you know that in the New Testament the word *worship* is translated from the Greek word *proskuneo*, meaning "to fall prostrate and kiss the feet of the one being worshiped"? Many people don't know this, and thus they miss what worship is truly all about. Indeed, most Muslims—though they are lost and following a false god—demonstrate a deeper reverence for Allah than most Christians do for the One True God. Wherever they are, devout Muslims get down on their knees and touch their foreheads to the ground as they pray.

How do you pray? How do you worship? Of course, God is our loving heavenly Father, and he can and will hear us whenever and wherever and in whatever position we pray. But we must understand that Scripture teaches us to bow down to worship the Lord as a sign of respect before the King of kings, as a way of practicing that we are in the very presence of almighty God.

Let's consider some verses (emphasis added).

- "The LORD, who brought you up from the land of Egypt with great power and with an outstretched arm, Him you shall fear, and to Him *you shall bow yourselves down*, and to Him you shall sacrifice" (2 Kings 17:36).
- "When Solomon finished praying, fire came down from heaven and consumed the burnt offering and the sacrifices, and the glory of the LORD filled the temple.

The priests could not enter the temple of the LORD because the glory of the LORD filled it. When all the Israelites saw the fire coming down and the glory of the LORD above the temple, *they knelt on the pavement with their faces to the ground, and they worshiped* and gave thanks to the LORD, saying, 'He is good; his love endures forever'" (2 Chronicles 7:1-3, NIV).

• "*Come, let us worship and bow down, let us kneel* before the LORD our Maker. For He is our God, and we are the people of His pasture and the sheep of His hand" (Psalm 95:6-7).

• "When Daniel knew that the document was signed, he entered his house . . . and *he continued kneeling on his knees* three times a day, praying and giving thanks before his God, as he had been doing previously" (Daniel 6:10).

• "He [Jesus] withdrew from them about a stone's throw, and *He knelt down* and began to pray." (Luke 22:41)

• "[The wise men] saw the child with his mother Mary, and *they bowed down and worshiped him*" (Matthew 2:11, NIV).

• "He [Jesus] went a little beyond them, and *fell on His face and prayed*, saying, 'My Father, if it is possible, let this cup pass from Me; yet not as I will, but as You will" (Matthew 26:39).

• "One of [the lepers whom Jesus miraculously healed], when he saw he was healed, came back, praising God in a loud voice. *He threw himself at Jesus' feet and thanked him*—and he was a Samaritan" (Luke 17:15-16, NIV).

- "For it is written, 'As I live, says the Lord, *every knee shall bow to Me*, and every tongue shall give praise to God'" (Romans 14:11).
- "God exalted him to the highest place and gave him the name that is above every name, that *at the name of Jesus every knee should bow*, in heaven and on earth and under the earth, and every tongue acknowledge that Jesus Christ is Lord, to the glory of God the Father" (Philippians 2:9-11, NIV).

These and other Scriptures clearly teach us the posture of worship. It was the practice of the people who discipled us to kneel to pray and praise God—in church and in their homes and in the homes of others—unless they were standing to sing or speak to the audience. Having seen them practice the presence of God—to believe and act as though Jesus was present in the room with them, as God promises—we have sought to follow their examples. And we encourage others to do so as well.

Is it worth getting legalistic about kneeling and demanding that everyone does it? Of course not. But we think you can see from the verses above that we serve a holy God—the King of kings—and because he deserves reverence, it makes sense to bow down before him.

We encourage you, therefore, to begin this practice, out of a pursuit of holiness and humility and love and respect for the Lord, not legalism. Set an example for your disciples. Explain to them why you do what you do. Then give them the freedom to follow this practice or not. In time, we think they will.

In time, they will enter into the very presence of the living God, and they will know it, and they will bow down. If you can gently encourage your congregation to understand this practice, all the better. Over the years as we have taught this practice from the Word of God, we have seen many people greatly blessed as they have truly come to understand the meaning and importance of honoring and respecting the almighty God in their own lives.

The Sacrifice of Praise

We grow more when we engage in true worship of the God who loves us and gave himself for us than we do with any other spiritual discipline. Yet when it comes to worship, the central problem in too many modern churches is that the average believer goes to church thinking, *What's in it for me?* He is not there primarily to please the Lord or honor him. He's often there to learn, to meet friends, to have fun, perhaps to eat. All those are good things, but they are not worship.

In Romans 12:1, Paul writes, "I urge you, brethren, by the mercies of God, to present your bodies a living and holy sacrifice, acceptable to God, which is your spiritual service of worship."

Many times we do not want to worship. Why? Because our minds are filled with distractions. Because we're too busy with other things, even "spiritual" things, that we think are more important. Because we are not in sync with God. Because we have sin in our lives. There are many reasons, but the same result—often we simply do not want to bow down and worship the God who loves us and made us and redeemed us.

That is precisely why Paul urges us—beseeches us, even—to approach worship as "a living and holy sacrifice."

What is a sacrifice? It is giving up something you don't want to give up. It is giving away your best to God, even if you don't want to—*especially* if you don't want to. Otherwise, it isn't a sacrifice, right?

So Paul, understanding our weaknesses and distractions, urges us to make a sacrifice of our time and thoughts and treasures and come before the Lord our God and give him what he deserves and what he desires—our praise and adoration.

Make no mistake: praise is a sacrifice.

In Hebrews 13:15, the writer says, "Through Him then, let us continually offer up a sacrifice of praise to God, that is, the fruit of lips that give thanks to His name."

And in 1 Peter 2:4-5, the apostle writes, "Coming to Him as to a living stone which has been rejected by men, but is choice and precious in the sight of God, you also, as living stones, are being built up as a spiritual house for a holy priesthood, to offer up spiritual sacrifices acceptable to God through Jesus Christ."

Let's face it. We are sinful, selfish, self-centered people. We want what we want when we want it.

Yes, we were created in God's image. But through sin we tend to think of ourselves as the center of the universe—even as believers, even as strong believers in Christ. Our prideful nature simply lies to us, trying to convince us to worship ourselves, rather than God.

So it's easy to decide we're too tired to go to church. Or when we're at church, that we should be involved in all kinds of different activities other than worship. Or during a worship service we want to *ask* God for things rather than praise him for who he is. Or we fall asleep. Or we get distracted by someone sitting near us. Or we feel judgmental toward people around us whose worship style is in some way different from our own. There are a million ways to be distracted, but the results are the same—we fail to worship God.

That is why we must see worship as a sacrifice. We must give him our best—beginning with our full time and attention and utter devotion—because he deserves it.

When you or your disciples don't "feel" like worshiping—when the enemy is attacking and distracting you—press forward and bring a "sacrifice of praise" to the Lord. As you do, God will help you break free of all those internal and external distractions and truly enter his presence and enjoy his company.

The paradox is that in giving we receive. In dying to ourselves and focusing totally and completely on him, we in fact become more alive than ever before.

Our Spiritual Birthright

What is truly amazing is that we are allowed to enter God's presence at all. In the Old Testament days, only the high priest could enter the presence of God and worship. No one else could enter God's presence. That limited people's ability to truly worship the Lord. But the Lord Jesus Christ through his finished work on the cross made it possible for every believer to become a priest and thus exercise his spiritual birthright. Consider the following verses:

- "As many as received Him, to them He gave the right to become children of God, even to those who believe in His name, who were born, not of blood nor of the will of the flesh nor of the will of man, but of God" (John 1:12-13).
- "This was in accordance with the eternal purpose which He carried out in Christ Jesus our Lord, in whom we have boldness and confident access through faith in Him" (Ephesians 3:11-12).
- "[The Lord] has made us to be a kingdom and priests to serve his God and Father" (Revelation 1:6, NIV).
- "You have made them to be a kingdom and priests to our God; and they will reign upon the earth" (Revelation 5:10).

Once we are born again, we enter the Kingdom of God as children of God. We suddenly become priests of the Most High God. We are now entitled—by the fact of our new birth and new position as priests—to enter the presence of God with boldness and confidence to worship him and magnify his name.

That's amazing.

Once, unless a person was born a Jewish Levite and became high priest and entered with the blood sacrifice of a perfect animal, he could not enter the Holy of Holies, the very presence of God, to worship him personally.

But now—if we are born again and thus enter covered by the blood of the Lord Jesus, the perfect sacrificial Lamb of God—we *may* enter the very presence of God to worship him personally.

Indeed, it is not just *acceptable* that we now bring a "sacrifice of praise" before the Lord; it is now the *spiritual birthright* of every disciple—the precious right and responsibility of every man and woman, boy and girl who knows the Lord—to reflect, radiate, and represent the beauty of the Lord Jesus Christ.

We urge you, therefore, to learn, practice, and teach your team true worship. Sing and praise and magnify the Lord. Teach them to take Communion, explaining what it means and its significance of purity and remembrance in worship. Teach them to pray and fast and put God first. Teach them to bow down on their knees before the Lord. Teach them the difference between Mary's worship and Martha's frenetic service and how to choose the better of the two. For in so doing you will be helping them please the very heart of God.

Silence and Solitude

It is vitally important to teach those you're investing in to take time away from the crowds and the busyness of life to practice silence and solitude and time alone with the Lord. This isn't an option; it's a top priority.

Life is busy. That's a given. People have many needs. The poor—financially and spiritually—will always be with us. And many people in ministry often have a pastor's heart. They want to care for every need. But it can't be done. And we'll harm ourselves trying. Thus, on a regular, consistent, disciplined basis, we must follow the model of Jesus. We must separate ourselves from the crowds and busyness of life and ministry and get away to be alone and quiet with the God who loves us and put this treasure in our jars of clay.

After all, true worship is not merely a function; it is a life-style. It should be practiced every day, not just on Sundays. Once you begin to learn the very spirit of worship, you are no longer a passive spectator. You become an active participant in the church. Ultimately, true worship flows from your personal experience with the Lord, not simply from a theoretical knowledge you may have of God. It is the by-product of our deep love and passion for the Lord, and it involves our spirits, our minds, our emotions—indeed, our entire being.

If you don't regularly get away to be alone with God, you'll never have the spiritual resources—the spiritual capital, if you will—to invest in the lives of others.

Moreover, if you don't practice silence and solitude and communion with the Lord, those you're discipling won't either. They will believe that working feverishly in ministry until all hours of the morning—without breaks, without time with God, without time alone, and without time with family and friends—is good and honorable and noble. But it isn't. It is foolish. You can't give 100 percent day in and day out.

What is sad, however, is how few people in ministry follow the example set by Jesus of getting away—not just from the crowds, but away from the disciples, as well. Don't make this mistake. Love the Lord your God with all your heart, soul, mind, and strength. This comes first. *Then* love your neighbors as yourself.

We recommend that you take some time to read through

the following verses and make notes on these key thoughts on solitude and silence as you do. We think you'll be fascinated by the picture Jesus paints for his disciples in the Gospel according to Mark. Hopefully God will show you how to apply this to your own life and to the lives of your disciples as well.

- "Very early in the morning, while it was still dark, Jesus got up, left the house and went off to a solitary place, where he prayed" (Mark 1:35, NIV).
- "Jesus withdrew with his disciples to the lake" (Mark 3:7, NIV).
- "The apostles gathered around Jesus and reported to him all they had done and taught. Then, because so many people were coming and going that they did not even have a chance to eat, he said to them, 'Come with me by yourselves to a quiet place and get some rest.' So they went away by themselves in a boat to a solitary place" (Mark 6:30-32, NIV).
- "After [Jesus] had left the crowd and entered the house, his disciples asked him about this parable" (Mark 7:17, NIV).
- "About four thousand were present. After he had sent them away, he got into the boat with his disciples and went to the region of Dalmanutha" (Mark 8:9-10, NIV).
- "After six days Jesus took Peter, James and John with him and led them up a high mountain, where they were all alone" (Mark 9:2, NIV).
- "They left that place and passed through Galilee. Jesus did not want anyone to know where they were, because he was teaching his disciples" (Mark 9:30-31, NIV).

- "As Jesus was sitting on the Mount of Olives opposite the temple, Peter, James, John and Andrew asked him privately" (Mark 13:3, NIV).
- "Going a little farther [away from his disciples, Jesus] fell to the ground and prayed that if possible the hour might pass from him" (Mark 14:35, NIV).

Worship is our spiritual birthright.

Communion with our God is absolutely essential.

So make time—regularly and consistently—to bring a "sacrifice of praise" to the Lord. Make time to get alone with the Lord and get on your knees before him in prayer, praise, worship, and reading and meditating on the Word of God. Jealously practice silence and solitude, even when you don't "feel" like it. For only hidden away with God can we come to know him more intimately and have something to say to those who look to us for leadership.

QUESTIONS

1. What does the Bible teach is the difference between praise and worship?

2. What makes worship so vital to our experience as disciples of Jesus Christ?

3. Do you worship God on your knees? Why or why not?

4. Does your church give you the opportunity to worship on your knees during the Sunday morning service? Why or why not?

5. What are some of the benefits of learning to bow down before the Living God?

6. What are the things that distract you from silence and solitude and true worship?

7. What specific steps can you take to make more time for God?

TESTIMONY:
JOEL C. ROSENBERG

My Orthodox Jewish great-grandparents on my father's side escaped the pogroms and persecution of the Jews in czarist Russia in the early years of the 1900s. They fled through Europe to the United States, eventually arriving in New York City. They settled in Brooklyn, where my father was born in June 1939, one of two boys.

My mother was born in Rome, New York, in December 1939 as the only child of a mother who was an English Methodist WASP (white, Anglo-Saxon, Protestant) and whose family came to America before the American Revolution, and a father whose family was German and came from Berlin before the World Wars. My maternal grandmother was a wonderful, sweet, gentle, and loving woman. However, my maternal grandfather, whom I never met, was a

violent alcoholic. He left his family not long after my mother
was born, so my mother was raised by her single mother.

Neither of my parents were believers when they met in
1964 in Syracuse, New York, and married in 1965. My dad
would have described himself as an "agnostic Orthodox Jew."
My mother would have described herself as an "agnostic
Methodist." They had both been raised in religious homes
but hadn't found God there. Indeed, they had been discouraged by their religious upbringings. Still, they wanted to
know God. They wanted to find him. They would take long
walks and talk about how to find God. They asked their
friends how to find God. They read the Qur'an. They read
the Bhagavad Gita. They read the New Testament. They
didn't understand any of them at first. But they kept seeking
the truth.

One day in 1973, after moving to the little town of
Fairport, New York—a suburb of Rochester—they happened
to visit a church where some young couples explained how
they had discovered how to know God in a real and personal
way. My mother was intrigued as these couples explained
what Jesus meant in John 3:3 when he said, "Truly, truly,
I say to you, unless one is born again he cannot see the kingdom of God." She didn't ever recall when she was growing up
in her church hearing John 14:6 when Jesus said, "I am the
way, and the truth, and the life; no one comes to the Father
but through Me." Nor did she recall ever hearing someone
tell her the most famous verse in the New Testament, John
3:16, in which Jesus said, "For God so loved the world, that
He gave His only begotten Son, that whoever believes in Him
shall not perish, but have eternal life." She was fascinated as

the couples explained how each of them had received Jesus Christ into their hearts by faith and thus been "born again," and how each of their lives had been transformed in the process.

As they explained Christ's offer of salvation as a free gift—not something we can earn or buy or merit on our own—something in my mom's heart quickened. She wanted her sins to be completely forgiven. She wanted to receive the righteousness of God offered to her through faith in Jesus. She wanted to be absolutely certain that when she died, she was going to spend eternity in heaven with God, not trapped in hell forever and ever with no way of escape. What's more, she wanted to experience God's peace and hope and joy in this life and was excited by the opportunity to meet people who said they had been "adopted" into God's family. That's what she wanted too. The couples explained that anyone who wanted to receive Jesus as Savior and Lord could come up to the front of the church and they would pray together. So as soon as the service was over, my mom bolted forward and prayed that very day to receive Christ as her Savior, and she assumed my father was right behind her.

My father, however, was not yet convinced. He was glad my mom had found something to make her happy, but he reminded her that he was Jewish and Jewish people don't believe in Jesus! But to his credit, he was willing to join a small-group Bible study that my mom had just learned about. Several couples (different ones from those who had spoken in church that Sunday morning) were planning to study the Gospel according to Luke. My mom was eager to learn about the life of Jesus and grow in her new faith. My father figured it would be an interesting intellectual exercise, an opportunity to get some of his questions about the New Testament answered.

What stunned him about what he was reading early on in the weekly Bible study, however, was that the angels were calling Jesus the Messiah. So were the demons. So were a growing number of people. And then one day Jesus made clear that he was, in fact, the Messiah. In my father's mind, there were only two logical possibilities for a person who claimed to be the Jewish Messiah: either he was, or he was not. My father, of course, assumed that Jesus was not the Messiah.

As he considered the situation more in depth, he decided that there were only two logical explanations for a man who claimed to be the Jewish Messiah but was not: either he *knew* he wasn't the Messiah and therefore was a liar, or he *thought* he was the Messiah but wasn't and thus was a lunatic. The problem was that as my father studied the life of Jesus—his love, his wisdom, his authoritative teaching, his miracles, his kindness and compassion, his forgiveness even for his enemies—my father couldn't conclude that Jesus was either a liar or a lunatic. Which left him with only one option: Jesus is the Lord.

After six months of careful study of the Bible and other Christian literature, and a lot of soul-searching and prayer, my father came home from work one night and gathered our little family in the kitchen and announced some big news: he had come to the conclusion that Jesus really is the Jewish Messiah and the Savior of the world. Therefore, he had prayed that evening on the bus ride home to receive Jesus into his heart by faith.

The year was 1973, and a dramatic spiritual revolution was under way in our family. I was only six years old, but this began my own spiritual journey. I started to see my parents' lives change in significant and wonderful ways. My father's volcanic and unpredictable temper dissipated. He softened and became much more loving and kind. He was developing a patience I'd never seen before, and I liked it. At the same time, my mother—who previously had been nearly paralyzed at times by fear and anxiety—was becoming a more peaceful and relaxed person. She was developing an inner joy that was noticeable and welcome! My parents weren't perfect, of course, but they were truly changing for the better in front of my eyes, and the only reason could be that what they said was true: Jesus was living inside them and transforming them from the inside out.

When I was eight, I received Jesus as my Savior, influenced significantly by my parents and the Sunday school teachers at the community church we began attending. I wasn't a huge fan of the Bible quizzes in Sunday school (known as "sword drills") or of the singing or crafts in vacation Bible school, but I loved those stories about the life of Jesus, and I desperately wanted to be certain that I was going to go to heaven when I died.

I can't say I became superspiritual in my elementary and middle school years, but I grew a little in my faith. My parents certainly began investing heavily in me. They prayed for me constantly, including praying for the girl I would eventually marry. They made sure I was active in our church, from the Boys' Brigade program (a Christian version of Boy Scouts) to our junior and senior high youth group. They drove me to whatever church events were going on and tried to encourage me over the years to develop a deeper hunger for Bible study and prayer. I was not a rebel growing up, but I did have my share of struggles. The short version is that it wasn't until about halfway through my junior year of high school that I really got excited and serious about my faith. But I am so grateful for my parents because they never stopped praying for me—sometimes with many tears—imploring God to protect me and lead me on the right path.

As my hunger for God intensified at the age of seventeen, my parents helped me develop an interest in missions and provided me a steady supply of Christian books and sermons on audiotape they found helpful. These included classics like *God's Smuggler* by Brother Andrew, *Green Leaf in Drought Time* by Isobel Kuhn, all of Jim and Elisabeth Elliot's books, *Born Again* by Chuck Colson, and a series of teaching tapes on discipleship and leadership by Dr. Howard Hendricks of Dallas Theological Seminary. By my senior year of high school, I finally decided to ask Christ to be Lord of my life, to lead me wherever he wanted me to go, to say whatever he wanted me to say, and to do whatever he wanted me to do. I helped found a prayer and Bible study group at Fairport High School called Christ for Life. We began actively sharing the gospel with fellow classmates and had the joy of seeing several pray to receive Christ.

My lifelong dream was to become a writer of novels and screenplays, so after graduation, I headed off to film school at Syracuse University (S.U.). There I met Nick DeCola and his soon-to-be wife, Debbi, both of whom worked with Campus Crusade for Christ.

Nick invited me to join his Bible study. He taught me how to do a better job sharing my faith, how to be clearer and more concise, and how to be more bold—not simply to wait for people to ask me spiritual questions but how to even initiate spiritual conversations. By God's grace, I had the opportunity to share the gospel with more than seventy people that first year. Nick took me to various Campus Crusade training conferences, and though it was like trying to take a drink of water from a fire hose, I tried to lap up everything I could. Then he encouraged me to go on a monthlong mission project in the summer of 1986 in what was then still known as the Soviet Union. I enthusiastically agreed (as did my parents), applied, and was accepted. That trip changed my life. I knew I wanted to be used by God to share the gospel all over the world and make disciples of all nations.

But I was going too fast for my own good. I was still very young. I didn't know how to pace myself. My heart was in the right place, but I was trying to serve God in my own power, not the power of the Holy Spirit, and I was on the fast track to spiritual burnout.

I met Dr. Koshy (everyone calls him simply "Koshy") briefly as a freshman at S.U., but it wasn't until my senior year that a friend and I actually attended the congregation he pastored, International Assembly, one Sunday morning. To be honest, it was a strange experience at first. We were among a small handful of Americans in the room. Everyone else was from another country—India, Pakistan, China, Ghana, Thailand, and various European and South

American countries too. Everyone was praying in their different native languages. They worshiped on their knees, which I
had never seen done before. And Koshy's Indian accent, style
of preaching, and message were so different from anything
I'd ever seen before.

When the service was over, I told my friend that this
wasn't the place for us and we should go. But at that moment,
Koshy came up to us and very kindly invited us over to lunch.
Before I could say no thank you, my friend accepted. I was
stuck. And looking back, I'm glad.

The first thing that hit me when we walked into the
Koshys' home was the wonderful smell of curry. But the next
and more important thing that hit me was the wonderful
sense of love and kindness and spiritual depth. It was so clear
that these people knew the living God, and instantly I wanted
to get to know them better. After lunch, Koshy sat down
with me in his dining room. It felt like he could see through
me. It felt like he could just see how sad and lonely I was
inside, desperate to know God more deeply and make him
known more effectively, but spiritually spent and without
any more reserves. Suddenly I began to sob uncontrollably.
Embarrassed and feeling foolish, I just wanted to leave or
hide. But as we spoke, I had a deep and unmistakable sense
that this man could help me, and wanted to, if I would only
let him take me under his wing. I sensed that the Lord was
telling me that he had brought me to Koshy the way he had
once introduced Timothy to the apostle Paul. Like Timothy,
I had potential, but I also had much more to learn. At that
time, I didn't need more opportunities to teach and lead.
Rather, I needed more opportunities to learn and follow.

For the next two years, Koshy and his wife invested in me and a small discipleship group they led. Lynn was part of that group, and together we learned and grew so much more than we could have ever imagined or expected. Yes, Dr. Koshy and his wife taught us biblical truth. But just as important, they modeled for us what a modern-day Acts 2:42 church could look like. We didn't just study Acts. We saw a church making disciples of all nations. We didn't just read about spiritual gifts. They helped us identify our gifts and develop them. One of my gifts is exhortation. So Koshy took me to speaking engagements and let me share my testimony and encourage people to live for Christ. He introduced me to international students and gave me opportunities to answer their spiritual questions. He helped me learn how to give sermons and gave me regular opportunities to speak before the church, even when I didn't do so well.

We didn't just read verses about biblical hospitality. We experienced it, and we were expected to practice it. We canvassed the campus, inviting students to come for friendship picnics. We helped cook. We drove to the apartments of international students and brought them mattresses and used furniture, since many seemed to have nothing but brand-new color TVs to help them learn English and combat their loneliness.

We didn't just read about prayer. We were part of a church that never held strategy meetings, only prayer meetings. Long ones. Prayer meetings that were conducted on our knees, for hours at a time. And we saw God answer in big, dramatic ways.

We got to help organize Billy Graham's Syracuse crusade in the spring of 1989 and organize an evening where non-Christian students could ask the great evangelist their toughest questions. It was exhilarating.

After Lynn and I graduated, married (Dr. Koshy performed our wedding ceremony), and moved to Washington, D.C., we wanted to model for others what we saw the Koshys and DeColas model for us—hospitality and a personal approach to spiritual investing. But the question was how. Sure, we knew how it worked on a college campus, but what about in a big city? What about when you're trying to pursue a career? What about when you need to build a marriage? What about when you add children to the mix? How is it possible?

Honestly, for our first seven years in Washington, we didn't do such a great job. We got involved in a young couples' fellowship class and joined a small-group Bible study, and these were wonderful experiences for us. But we also tried to find a ministry for us and ended up volunteering for all kinds of different ministries in our church, from serving in the nursery and teaching Sunday school for young children to serving on the missions committee and developing an evangelism training class. Unfortunately, we found ourselves increasingly exhausted and unfulfilled. These weren't sinful activities, obviously, but something wasn't clicking for us. Something was wrong.

Eventually, one of our pastors took us aside and suggested that we not keep stretching ourselves so thin. Moreover, he asked us if we would simply be willing to begin making a few disciples, with the prayerful goal of helping develop a culture of discipleship in our church from the bottom up, since he felt he had been unsuccessful in developing such a culture from the top down. We agreed to chew on that for a bit, and one day in the summer of 1997, we decided to drive up to

Syracuse and spend a weekend visiting the DeColas and the
Koshys and seek their counsel. Both couples were very gentle
and encouraging, but both asked essentially the same question: In all the other ministries we had been involved with
since getting married, had we been making disciples? We
rattled off the list of various things we had been doing, but
again they said, "Yes, yes, but are you making any disciples?"

We thought about it and looked at each other and realized
that the painful answer was "Not really." We had encouraged a few younger believers along the way, but we weren't
intentionally and systematically taking any younger believers
under our wings and specifically investing in them.

Dr. Koshy then gave us his prescription: "I'd suggest you go
back to Washington and stop trying to be busy doing so many
different things. Just start praying for the Lord to bring one
young man for you to disciple, Joel, and one young woman for
you to disciple, Lynn. Nothing more. Just do that, and I think
you'll see the Lord bless you in many, many ways."

As we drove home, we decided the Koshys and DeColas
were right, and so was our pastor. We had sort of forgotten
the basics of the Great Commission, and our disobedience to
this central element of Jesus' heart was likely the reason we
felt so spiritually barren and discouraged.

We began praying together and with Lynn's mom. We
had only been praying together for a few weeks when out
of the blue I got a call from that same pastor at our church.
"Joel," he said, "a young man who recently visited our church
just trusted Christ a few months ago. He's looking for someone to answer his questions and help him grow deeper in his

faith. I thought perhaps you might be interested in meeting with him. How about it?"

I was elated. I called the guy, a young professional who worked at the United States Patent and Trademark Office. His name was John Black, and we met for a meal at a nearby restaurant. After asking him to share with me his spiritual journey to that point and what he was looking for, I instantly felt comfortable with him. I sensed this was the Lord's answer to my prayers and asked John if he'd like to begin to meet regularly, every Tuesday night for Bible study and prayer and answers to his many questions. He eagerly agreed and we were off to the races!

Almost simultaneously, Lynn received a call from her younger sister, Susan, who had prayed to receive Christ a few years before. Now Susan wanted to go deeper in her faith and wondered if Lynn would be willing to meet with her on a regular basis to answer her questions and take her deeper. Lynn was thrilled. She too sensed this was the Lord's answer to her prayers, and they began meeting weekly as well.

These were exciting answers to prayer. I loved the opportunity to help a new believer grow in his faith, but I also loved welcoming John into our home the way the DeColas and the Koshys had welcomed us. Lynn would make dinner for our family, and I'd invite John to join us. He'd usually arrive around 6 p.m., and our young boys loved to play with John as Lynn was finishing preparations for the meal. They treated him like an older brother. (Caleb started calling him "John Black John Black," and that nickname has stuck to this day.) Over dinner we would laugh and tell stories and get to know each other better. After dinner, John and I would help clean up the kitchen and then we'd retreat to the family room for our study and prayer time while Lynn took the boys upstairs and got them ready for bed. I never ceased to be amazed or encouraged by John's voracious hunger to study God's Word. What's more, I appreciated that he asked a million questions—and not just "spiritual" questions but questions about how to handle finances, how to handle dating relationships, how to handle problems with coworkers, and so on. Often, it would be closing in on midnight and he'd still be asking questions. Rather than feeling drained, I usually found myself energized by the conversations. Still, sometimes I would have to close my Bible and say, "Okay, that's it, John. I'm going to bed. Let's pick this up next week."

But discipleship didn't just happen once a week. We would e-mail each other during the week with prayer requests and answers to prayer. We shared books with each other. We occasionally went to conferences together, including one at Dallas Theological Seminary to hear Dr. Howard Hendricks (a tremendously gifted professor we deeply loved and admired) speak. We volunteered to help with various ministry projects at our church, including outreaches to the poor.

Before long, the Lord brought a few more young men along who wanted to join the discipleship group. Some were as hungry to grow in their faith as John. Others, we would realize over time, just wanted a social group but were not serious about growing spiritually. Together, we learned how to disciple others, how to help other young men study God's Word, develop a better prayer life, handle relationships with the opposite sex in a more godly way, manage their finances

more responsibly, and begin to share the gospel and participate in other church ministries.

I wish I could tell you this was all happening at a time
when my life was quiet. But the opposite was true. I'd never
been busier, personally or professionally. This was between the
years 1997 and 2000. I had just worked as a senior advisor on
Steve Forbes's presidential campaign in 1996 and at the time
was serving as the communications director for Steve's newly
formed and rapidly growing political grassroots organization.
Then I served as deputy campaign manager on Steve's 2000
presidential campaign. During this time, Lynn and I were raising three children, Caleb, Jacob, and Jonah (Noah didn't come
along until 2004). Also during this time, Lynn's discipleship
group was expanding beyond Susan, and she was soon discipling six women, even while she was investing heavily in our
sons and helping me with my fast-moving political career.

Believe me, we never planned to be discipling more than
one person at a time. For me, just discipling John Black for
a few years would have been wonderful enough. For Lynn,
just discipling her sister would also have been wonderful
enough. But God had other plans. He made it clear that he
wanted us to invest in others. He didn't tell us that at first.
If he had, we might have gotten scared or overwhelmed. But
as we were faithful in a few things, he gave us more to do.
He also gave us the strength and the joy and the eagerness
to invest in more men and women. We couldn't have done
any of it without his direction and without his strength, nor
would we have wanted to. But our goals had changed. We
were no longer trying to be busy in ministry. We were just
trying to be faithful in following Jesus wherever he took us.

He doesn't take everyone down the same road, but in our case he expanded our opportunities to invest.

We found the key to fruitfulness lay in two words: *priorities* and *synergy*. Fulfilling the Great Commandments and the Great Commission became our top priorities, even as we raised our kids. And we made sure we integrated our marriage and children in this ministry of discipleship. The secret, we found, was doing more by doing less and doing it better. For us in those early years, discipleship wasn't a drain on our marriage or family. It was a wellspring of new, enduring friendships and lots of fun.

Fortunately, the Lord helped us develop a schedule that worked for our family, though that schedule has changed over the years. In those early years, every Tuesday night at 7 p.m., five young men from our church came over to our home as part of a men's discipleship team. Every other Thursday night, six women from our church came over as part of a women's discipleship team Lynn led. Lynn prepared a meal. The rest of us helped out, setting the table, making salads, pouring drinks, and so forth. Around 7:45 p.m. on Tuesdays, Lynn put the kids to bed, read the Bible to them, and prayed with them. Meanwhile, the men and I had dinner and shared prayer requests. Lynn then read or caught up on bills or responded to e-mails. Starting around 8:30, I led the men in an inductive study of Scripture, asking lots of questions and giving the guys the chance to ask their own. Around 9:30 p.m., we got on our knees and prayed for specific needs God had put on our hearts.

We usually wound up around 10:15 p.m., at which time the guys could head home if they wanted. Often, one or two stayed until eleven—sometimes later—asking questions about their careers, challenges in ministry, dreams for the future, and relationships with family and friends. Lynn often came down and joined us after the "official" meeting was over. The guys seemed to really enjoy getting a woman's perspective on life and ministry. On Thursday nights, the roles were reversed. I put the kids to bed, reading the Bible to them and praying with them and learning about their day. Lynn led the Bible study, and occasionally I joined the women after their time of prayer. As with the men, the women enjoyed getting a man's perspective on their questions about life and ministry.

In addition to weekly meetings, I had one-on-one meetings with each guy at least once a month—and twice a month with John Black, who was my apprentice and was learning how to lead a discipleship group. Lynn met one-on-one with the women every other week. During these one-on-one times, we had lunch or dinner together, caught up on prayer requests, and discussed ministry development, family needs, personal and professional goals, and opportunities. We encouraged each other and kept each other accountable on issues like personal holiness and daily quiet times. Again, just as with my original discipleship relationship with John Black, I tried to phone or e-mail each guy at least once or twice a week, often more. We also planned fellowship times together—often in combination with Lynn and the women's discipleship group—including game nights, parties, and Saturday outings. Each Memorial Day weekend, we organized a camping, hiking, or beach retreat, a time to get away from the pressures of Washington and spend more time together in fellowship, Bible study, and prayer. In short, we tried to reproduce what the DeColas and the Koshys had modeled for us.

Lynn and I also strongly encouraged each person we discipled to serve in a ministry in the church God had called them to and to get spiritual input, teaching, and advice from other church leaders, not just us. We encouraged them to find new ways to share their faith and invest in younger believers. For three successive summers, we took our kids, Lynn's mom, and members of our discipleship teams on two-week mission trips to Spain, Morocco, and Gibraltar to share Christ with North African Arab Muslims and distribute the Arabic-language New Testaments and Arabic translations of the *JESUS* film. Most of us, honestly, were terrified the first time we went on such a mission trip. But that was good for us. We needed to get outside our comfort zones and share the gospel with people of other cultures and religions. We learned to pray more passionately when we were doing ministry we'd never done before. We also learned to lean on one another—and work our way through conflicts with one another—and in the process we grew much closer to each other and to the Lord.

As these men and women grew deeper in their faith, we encouraged them to begin praying for younger believers to invest in. Some were faithful to do this right away and began to disciple others. Others weren't ready and didn't start making disciples until several years later.

One morning when we were on vacation in Colorado, I sensed in my prayer time that God was telling us to bring these groups to an end. We loved each member like brothers and sisters, but the Lord didn't want them to become dependent on us. He wanted them to be dependent on him. I told Lynn what the Lord was telling me, and while she didn't like the idea at first, she knew it was from the Lord. At our next meeting when we got back home, we announced the groups would be winding down. Some were supportive and eager to see where the Lord was going to take them next. Some, however, were angry with us, feeling like we were abandoning them. We assured them that we had no such intent and would still be there for them individually. But we also told them that when the Lord speaks, we need to obey or it is sin.

What was really exciting to me was to see what the Lord did in the lives of those young twentysomethings in the months and years that followed the end of our discipleship groups.

- "John Black John Black" came to work for my company for a few years, traveling with me all throughout Israel and the Middle East and all over the United States and Canada preaching the gospel and teaching the Word of God. Then he went on to work for our church for a while, helping in the missions ministry, and later moved to Texas and earned a master's degree from Dallas Theological Seminary. He loved every minute of his time there (especially studying under Dr. Hendricks), and I loved going down there from time to time to visit him and then taking Lynn and the boys down to see him graduate. All this time he continued discipling young men and has a real passion for seeing men deeply rooted in the Word and committed to the

Great Commission. After graduation, he studied at
another university overseas for a year, and there he met
a wonderful young Christian woman from Germany,
fell in love, and married. What a fun answer to prayer!
At their request, I had the great joy of officiating
at their wedding and preaching the gospel to their
unsaved friends! Today they are in full-time Christian
ministry overseas and seeing the Lord use them to
advance the Kingdom in so many exciting ways.

- Susan has grown so much in the Lord, became a leader
in the short-term missions ministry at our church,
and went on (and co-led) more mission trips than I
can remember. She married Dan, a wonderful young
Lebanese Christian man she met at our church and
got to know better on a mission trip to Brazil. I later
helped disciple Dan, and in time he joined the staff of
our church and is now involved in the media ministry
and part of the worship team. They are raising four
wonderful children, all of whom know the Lord, and
are seeing God use them to lead others to Christ and
grow in their faith.

- Edward is another one of the guys I was discipling. He
fell in love with Kailea, whom Lynn was discipling,
and the two of them eventually got married. Edward
became so excited about discipleship that he resigned
his job in the corporate world and traveled with Dr.
Koshy around the world for the better part of a year
to go deeper in his faith and learn how to be a pastor
with a heart to reach the nations. Eventually he came
on staff with my company, and in 2006, he helped

Lynn and me start our nonprofit organization, The Joshua Fund (www.joshuafund.net), and served as our first director of operations. He traveled with me to Israel, Jordan, Turkey, and all over the United States preaching and teaching and sharing God's heart for Israel and her neighbors. He continues to serve on the board of The Joshua Fund ministry to this day. To our great joy, Edward also went on to become a wonderful pastor of a thriving congregation of about four hundred young people just outside Washington, D.C. He also serves as a chaplain at a nearby university and is passionate about discipling men and teaching them to disciple others.

- Kailea not only got married to Edward but she also played a key role in helping us launch The Joshua Fund and for a while served on our board. She served for a long time on the leadership team of the Global Impact ministry at our church. In recent years she has become the director of cross-cultural ministries with the church. Along the way, she has helped recruit, train, and deploy dozens of leaders of short-term mission teams who have taken hundreds upon hundreds of young people overseas to share the gospel and encourage local congregations in a variety of different cultures. Even as a wife and the mother of two adorable little girls, Kailea has continued personally discipling women and helping them to spiritually reproduce their lives as well.

- Two of the other women Lynn was discipling—Amy and Lori—took a class together at our church about reaching the Muslim world with the gospel. Within the class, they soon discovered five other single women with a similar heart for the Muslim world. That group of women, with Amy and Lori leading, eventually felt led to resign from their jobs and go to the mission field—some for six months and some for a full year. Amy went on to help us start The Joshua Fund, served on our board, and helped disciple many women at our church before the Lord took her home to heaven in April 2009. Lori, meanwhile, became a tremendous prayer warrior, faithfully praying for so many people and encouraging many others in their faith. She married a wonderful believer and moved to Texas, where they have continued to be involved in missions and local ministry, too.

- Wendy, another young woman Lynn was discipling, went on staff with our church for a number of years, investing in high school students. She married Colin, who at the time was on staff with Young Life. Together, they joined a young couples' discipleship group we led before the Lord gave them government jobs, moved them overseas, and gave them all kinds of new opportunities to share their faith and disciple others around the globe.

- Most of the others in those original groups are still faithfully walking with the Lord and serving him fruitfully around the world, and we stay in touch with them as best we can. Some, however, faded away, and we never heard from them again. We pray for them still from time to time. It's sad, but it happens.

Looking back, I can certainly say I have made a number of mistakes. I certainly wasn't the greatest disciple maker with those who bore fruit or with those who began to backslide. The truth was I was learning by doing. There are times I wish I could go back and do things over again. I would handle some opportunities and some conflicts very differently now. If I could replay those relationships, I would be more firm with some of the guys I thought weren't taking their faith seriously enough. With others I would be gentler and more forgiving. I would give more time to all of them and try to be a better listener and a better friend. The good news is, none of these folks were ever really my disciples or Lynn's. They were, and are, Jesus' disciples. We just had the chance to invest in them for a season, and imperfect though we were, we did the best we could. We don't take any credit for any of the fruit God has borne through these dear ones. Nor can we shoulder the blame for any of their failures. We're just trying to give you a picture of how we approached discipleship in the early years of this ministry and some of what happened.

That said, life is about seasons, and not every season is the same. Neither Jesus nor Paul gave us a formula for discipleship. Nor did the Koshys or the DeColas. Rather, they gave us models to learn from, and we have sought to apply these principles in our own unique environments. Thus, in the years that followed those first two discipleship groups, we led a number of other types of groups. For example:

- One year, Lynn and I co-led (with Edward and Kailea) a discipleship group for four couples, three of whom were newly married. Discipling singles, we learned that year, had been relatively easy by comparison. The singles had much more discretionary time and often more energy than young couples. But this group was good for us. We took them through an early draft of this book you're reading, *The Invested Life*. We tried to invest in their marriages as well as teach them to make discipleship a priority in their increasingly busy lives. To our great joy, each of the couples went on to develop a real heart for the Great Commission and began making disciples despite many challenges.

- Sometimes Lynn and I have had the opportunity to invest in young couples we helped lead to faith in Jesus Christ. What a joy to help new believers develop a firm foundation for their new faith!

- Other times, we've had the joy of helping to disciple young couples who were preparing to go on staff with a parachurch ministry. One year, for example, we took several couples who were newly on staff with The Joshua Fund through *The Invested Life*. It was a joy to get to know these couples more deeply and to help them see the principles that had become central to our own lives and that we were hoping to establish as part of this new ministry. Another time, we invested several months in a young couple who were raising financial support to go on full-time staff with Campus Crusade for Christ (now called "Cru").

- Over the past few years, Lynn and I have been blessed to be able to invest in a couple who came to faith in Jesus Christ from a Muslim background. The wife was raised in Iran as a Shia Muslim. Her

husband was raised as a nominal Christian in South
Korea. He actually converted to Shia Islam to marry
her. But then she had a supernatural encounter
with Jesus Christ, started attending our church, and
became a very devoted Christian. Stunned by her
transformation, the husband eventually gave his heart
to Christ and became eager to grow in his faith. Lynn
and I were introduced to them, and after they asked
if we would disciple them, we prayed about it and felt
a peace from the Lord to say yes. Over time, we have
had the joy of baptizing both of them and their two
sons who have come to Christ. We got to pray with
them for the salvation of the wife's Iranian parents.
Amazingly, both of her parents eventually had visions
of Christ and became Christ followers. What a thrill!
it was to baptize them, too! This family has become so
hungry to know Jesus and make him known. They've
gone on one family mission trip after another. They
share their faith regularly in their neighborhood and
their workplaces. They have now matured in their
faith to the point where they are discipling others and
using the principles they learned in *The Invested Life*.
Given the sensitivities of being Muslim Background
Believers, I am choosing not to use their names here.
But we have been so blessed by their friendship. The
husband and I have taken young pastors and ministry
leaders through *The Invested Life*. Lynn and the wife
have, likewise, taught the principles of this book to
young women eager to begin making disciples. What
a great joy they have been to us personally, and what a

joy to see them walking close to Jesus and being used
by him to make disciples of other nations, too.

Some of the folks we have invested in really got it and
put these principles into practice right away and saw God
produce some fruit. Others actually saw a lot of fruit. Still
others didn't seem to embrace these principles as quickly or
as devoutly as we hoped they would. Perhaps we were not the
most effective teachers. Perhaps we didn't model the material
as well as we should have. Perhaps we offended some of them
with our own flaws and imperfections and inadvertently
made it difficult for them to get excited about the biblical
centrality of making disciples of all nations. Perhaps some
simply didn't have ears to hear what the Spirit was saying to
them. Perhaps some will eventually develop those spiritual
ears but weren't ready at the time we were teaching them.
Whatever the case, we were honored to be involved in the
lives of all of them and to pray for them faithfully, and we
learned a great deal from each of the people we have tried
to disciple. Anything good that has developed in their lives
is because of God, not because of us, and we rejoice in it.
Anything that didn't go well likely had multiple reasons, and
hopefully people will forgive us for the mistakes we made.
But still we rejoice in all of it and hope Jesus gives us more
opportunities to invest in more people until he takes us home
to be with him.

I realize I'm running a risk here of drawing too much
attention to the people we have invested in and the results we
have seen. But please understand my intention isn't to draw
attention to us, per se.

My desire is to give you a snapshot of how we have approached the process of living "the invested life." I hope you're getting a sense of how we have tried to put into practice that which we have seen and heard from the Koshys and the DeColas. Lynn and I haven't always invested in people's lives in the same ways. We haven't always used the same methods. We haven't always had the same results. Therefore, we're not recommending a specific methodology of discipleship. Rather, we are recommending that you commit yourself to ask Jesus to show you how to live the invested life where you are. Study the Scriptures about discipleship carefully. Prayerfully seek a Paul to invest in you. Prayerfully seek a Barnabas (or two or three) to befriend and encourage you. Then prayerfully seek a Timothy, a younger believer into whom you can invest. Ask the Lord to show you how best to do the investing. Hopefully some of the methods we have shared in this book will be helpful. As we read in Psalm 23, the Lord is your Shepherd, right? He will lead you. He will guide you. He will comfort and encourage and direct you. Stay connected to him and don't let yourself grow weary, and in due time you will bear fruit that will last.

King Solomon once wrote, "There is an appointed time for everything. And there is a time for every event under heaven" (Ecclesiastes 3:1). Likewise, Solomon wrote that the Lord "has made everything beautiful in its time" (Ecclesiastes 3:11, NIV). Following Jesus has led us to making disciples. So long as we let him choose the time, the place, the people, and the method—and so long as we trust him for the results and recognize they are all his—then discipleship is a beautiful thing. It certainly has been for us. Being involved with a lifestyle of discipleship has been a great blessing to us individually and as a family. We've found that it's a two-way street. We not only invested in others, but to our surprise and great appreciation, they in turn invested back in us and our children. It was the people I referenced above, along with our family, who encouraged me to write my first novel and weave the gospel into it. They were the ones who prayed for the Lord to bless these books and use them to open doors to preach the gospel and teach the Word of God, here at home and around the world. They helped us start The Joshua Fund, and they continue to help staff and govern this ministry. These dear ones have wept with us when life became hard and painful. And they laughed and rejoiced with us when we saw God do mighty miracles.

We never expected any of it. The Lord could take it all away now and we would still praise his holy name. Lynn and I and our boys are trying not to live for the results. We are trying to live for Jesus. We don't want him to be disappointed with us when we stand before him face-to-face. We don't want him to wonder why we didn't love him enough to obey the Great Commission to "go therefore and make disciples of all the nations." We want to hear from his lips what you want to hear as well: "Well done, good and faithful servant! You have been faithful with a few things; I will put you in charge of many things. Come and share your master's happiness!" (NIV).

Through the years, we have developed a set of core principles that we use in our disciple making. Many of these principles are explained in detail elsewhere in this book. But here's a short list for easy reference:

- **Integrate marriage, family, and ministry.** If you're married, serve with your spouse as often as possible. If you have kids, include them in your disciple making. Eat meals as a family with the people you're investing in. Go together on mission trips as a family. Don't let the invested life divide and conquer you. Don't let it exhaust you. Let it bring you together to have a stronger, sweeter marriage and more time with your kids!
- **Listen and pray.** People need someone to listen to their troubles and pray with them and for them. Don't let your objective be just to teach people. Don't just try to get through some curriculum. Don't simply be goal-oriented. Be people-oriented. Listen to them. Love them. And keep loving them even when you discover how troubled and broken they really are.
- **Lead leaders.** Definitely disciple new believers. They can become leaders. But also focus on faithful, reliable men and women who can and will train others. Keep your eye on developing a ministry of multiplication.
- **Create a warm, safe place.** Invite people to your home, however small or large it may be, on a regular basis. Let people come and vent and recharge. Let them kick their shoes off, and you'll find they'll open their hearts as well. Too many people forget the power of biblical hospitality. Let's not be among them.
- **Focus on the Great Commandments.** Build a team that truly loves each other. Remember: they will know we are Jesus' disciples by our love.
- **Focus on the Great Commission.** Don't build a social club. Build a team that is committed to changing the

world. Teach your team to preach the gospel. Teach them to teach the Word. Take them on mission trips. Then set them loose!

May the Lord bless you beyond what you can hope for, dream of, or imagine as you prayerfully find the answers to those two simple questions: Who is investing in you? And in whom are you investing?

CHAPTER NINE

TRACK YOUR PROGRESS

Be diligent in these matters; give yourself wholly
to them, so that everyone may see your progress.
THE APOSTLE PAUL (1 TIMOTHY 4:15, NIV)

Paul encouraged Timothy to be so focused on pleasing God and making disciples that "everyone may see your progress." This should be your mission as well.

Remember your two basic goals as a disciple maker:

1. Help people obey the Great Commandments.
2. Help people fulfill the Great Commission.

A Discipleship Checklist

In pursuit of these two basic goals, consider a list of practical guideposts to help you in your ongoing ministry of discipleship.

It's a long list. But fear not.

261

Don't get overwhelmed. Just take things one day at a time, one step at a time, so that you and others can see steady, measurable progress.

- **A good disciple maker practices hospitality (Romans 12:9-13).**
  - Because he believes the home is one of the best places to do ministry, he invites those he's investing in into his home.
  - He invites missionaries and other Christian workers into his home, even at times when it is inconvenient.
  - He invites strangers and nonbelievers into his home to love them and lead them to Christ.
  - He provides home-cooked meals.
  - He creates a warm, safe, godly environment in which his team can retreat from the world for love and encouragement.
  - He includes his team in family events, such as birthday parties, celebrations, and game nights.

- **A good disciple maker cares for the whole person (Luke 2:52).**
  - Just as "Jesus kept increasing in wisdom and stature, and in favor with God and men"—that is, in all areas of life: mental, physical, spiritual, and social—an effective discipler cares for all areas of his team's life and faith.

- He wants to help each of his team members to *be* a man after God's own heart, not simply to *do* things for God.

- He listens to and knows his team's testimonies.

- He regularly asks about his team's friendships and offers biblical guidance and practical help.

- He consistently asks about his team's families and offers biblical guidance and practical help for loving their parents and families and helping *them* come to know Christ, grow in their faith, and handle the difficult problems and challenges they face.

- He regularly asks about his team's finances and offers biblical guidance and practical help to tithe and give to the Lord, establish an effective budget, get out of debt, build up savings, and invest for the future.

- He regularly asks his team members about their time management and offers them biblical guidance and practical help to evaluate how they spend their time, establish priorities, and do more by doing less and doing it better.

- He keeps his team accountable in the areas of physical purity, courtship, marriage, and personal relationships.

- He knows his team's birthdays.

- He is there for his team members at key moments in their lives—good and bad—including birthdays, weddings, and funerals for their family members or friends.

- He prays *for* them.

- He prays *with* them.

- He helps his team discover that our God is a prayer-hearing and a prayer-answering God.

- He doesn't ask too *much* of them—that is, he doesn't overwhelm his disciples with so much homework and so many projects and assignments that they are either drowning or are neglecting essentials such as their schoolwork, jobs, or family relationships.

- He doesn't ask too *little* of them—that is, he is helping them aim high and train hard to be useful and effective players in the most exciting and dramatic spiritual revolution in the history of the world.

- He does not abandon his team when they make mistakes, sin, or fail—indeed, he stands by them and tries to help them repent, experience God's forgiveness, make appropriate restitution, and again walk humbly with the Lord.

- At the same time, he sets the highest possible biblical standards for his team, and if a member has no intention of truly following the Lord, he has the courage to gently but firmly inform the disciple that he needs to get serious or, in a worst-case scenario, part ways from the team.

- **A good disciple maker helps his team master the basics of the faith (1 Timothy 4:1-5).**
  - He makes sure each member of his team knows Jesus Christ in a real and personal way.
  - He makes sure each member of his team has the assurance of salvation.
  - He makes sure his team are all baptized as true followers of Jesus Christ and baptizes them himself if needed.
  - He encourages them to have daily quiet time in the Word and with the Lord Jesus in prayer first thing in the morning.
  - He encourages them to read, meditate on, memorize, and observe the Word of God on a daily basis.
  - He teaches his team to observe all that Jesus commanded by leading them through a systematic study of the Word of God, beginning with at least one of the Gospels.
  - He makes sure his team is grounded in solid biblical theology.
  - He teaches his disciples to live by faith that Jesus is always with them and has all authority in heaven and on earth.

- He helps his team to understand the centrality, purposes, and functions of the New Testament church, where followers of Christ were worshiping God in spirit and truth, preaching the gospel, making disciples of all nations and cultures, planting other churches, and continually devoting themselves to (1) the apostles' teaching, (2) fellowship, (3) the breaking of bread (Communion), and (4) prayer (see Acts 2:42).

- He attends church, conferences, and retreats with his team.

- He encourages his team to read Christian books he has found useful over the years.

- He encourages his team to listen to recordings of sermons and other messages by Christian leaders he has found helpful over the years.

- He practices the spiritual disciplines of silence and solitude and encourages his team to take regular, consistent time away from ministry to be alone with God.

- He helps his team discover and develop their unique spiritual gifts (see Romans 12; 1 Corinthians 12–14; Ephesians 4).

- **A good disciple maker helps his team learn to share their faith with all men everywhere (1 Timothy 2:1-8).**

  - He teaches his team how to share their testimonies in a brief, compelling, and winsome manner.

- He teaches his team how to share their faith using a brief, concise explanation of the gospel, based on the Word of God.

- He teaches his team how to answer both common and difficult questions that nonbelievers ask.

- He shows his team how to share their faith by taking them out to public places, striking up conversations, and asking people if they would like to learn how to have a personal relationship with God.

- He sends his team out to share their faith and observes them in the process.

- He reviews his team's performance, answers their questions, and offers constructive, practical, positive advice for doing better the next time.

- He teaches his team how to teach *other* believers how to share *their* faith and take this third generation of disciples out to practice *their* new evangelism skills.

- He takes his team out to participate in a wide variety of ministry service projects to help them encounter many different experiences, scenarios, and the myriad of questions they inspire.

- He leads short-term mission projects to other nations to show his team how to share their faith cross-culturally and to help them develop a vision for reaching the world for Christ.

- He leads his team in prayer for the persecuted church and helps them see the cost of being a true disciple of Jesus Christ.

- **A good disciple maker helps his team learn how to make disciples of all nations (Matthew 28:18-20; 2 Timothy 2:2).**

  - He teaches his team the centrality of discipleship in God's plan and purpose for our lives.

  - He is a loving, compassionate, wise, and winsome model of biblical discipleship.

  - He helps his team gain confidence in cross-cultural ministry, rooting out any hint of anxiety, fear, prejudice, or racism that may lie (even buried) within a disciple's heart.

  - He prays with his team to find "faithful men" to disciple who will be "able to teach others also."

  - He provides sound biblical and practical advice and encouragement as his team begins to disciple others.

  - He answers tough questions team members have during the course of discipling others.

  - He looks for opportunities in which he and his team can speak about the centrality of discipleship with other believers and share personal experiences and lessons.

- He prays with and counsels his team with regard to God's long-term will for their lives and ministries, including marriage, family, and career (marketplace ministry or full-time vocational Christian service).

- **A good disciple maker helps his team members become wise spiritual leaders (1 Timothy 3:1-10).**

  - He helps his team understand biblical leadership by modeling servant leadership.

  - He chooses a member of his team to be his apprentice and gives him opportunities to plan and lead Bible studies and prayer meetings.

  - He encourages his team to meet with other believers for prayer and accountability.

  - He teaches his team how to teach a Bible study and gives them opportunities to practice.

  - After leading his team on one or more short-term mission trips, he equips them to lead (or co-lead) various trips themselves.

  - He encourages his team to study the examples of famous spiritual and secular leaders to evaluate their strengths, weaknesses, and secrets of success.

  - He helps his team develop a sense of eternal destiny and a courage and fearlessness about being fully engaged in the Lord's global spiritual revolution.

- He helps his team learn to persuade others to follow Christ more faithfully, partly through biblical exhortation and partly through modeling a personal lifestyle of God's love and vision for ministry.

- He gently corrects his team when they make mistakes and carefully helps them combat spiritual pride, arrogance, and insensitivity to others.

- He helps his team members pace themselves— to simultaneously avoid spiritual burnout and spiritual complacency.

- He actively encourages his team to involve other older, wiser men of God in their lives so that they don't become overly dependent on one person and one view and style of ministry.

- He equips his team members to have lives and ministries of their own.

- He eventually *encourages* his team members to go out and have lives and ministries of their own.

- He stays in touch with his disciples (even when he no longer meets with them regularly), writes to them, and—as the Lord permits—visits them personally to help them grow in the faith, make new disciples, and establish vibrant new ministries.

Give an Account

In Luke 9:1-2, 10, we read that when the disciples returned to Jesus after being sent out to "proclaim the kingdom of God," they "gave an account to Him of all that they had done."

One exercise you might consider doing with your team is taking some time each year, perhaps in January, to reflect on what God is doing in and through you and how well you're obeying the Great Commandments and the Great Commission. Then give God an account.

Spiritual Audit: The Great Commandments

LOVING GOD

On a scale of 1 to 10, how am I doing in the following areas? What are my goals for the coming year?

- Consistent daily prayer time with God.
    *Score (1-10):*_____
    My goal for the new year: _____
    _____

- Consistent daily Bible study time with God/depth of Bible knowledge.
    *Score (1-10):*_____
    My goal for the new year: _____
    _____

- Consistent weekly worship time/depth of understanding of biblical worship.
    *Score (1-10):*_____
    My goal for the new year: _____
    _____

- Physical and mental purity.
    Score (1-10):_____
  My goal for the new year: _____

  _____

LOVING OTHERS

On a scale of 1 to 10, how am I doing in the following areas? What are my goals for the coming year?

- Loving my family and friends.
    Score (1-10):_____
  My goal for the new year: _____

  _____

- Consistent practice of hospitality.
    Score (1-10):_____
  My goal for the new year: _____

  _____

- Consistent acts of service.
    Score (1-10):_____
  On a separate page, list some acts of service for others you've done this past year.
  My goal for the new year: _____

  _____

- Turning the other cheek.
    Score (1-10):_____
  On a separate page, list some times you've turned the other cheek and not repaid evil for evil this past year.
  My goal for the new year: _____

  _____

Spiritual Audit: The Great Commission

EVANGELISM

On a scale of 1 to 10, how am I doing in the following areas? What are my goals for the coming year?

- Confidence in sharing my faith in Christ and leading someone to make a decision to trust Christ as Savior.

  *Score (1-10):*_____

  My goal for the new year: _____

  _____

- Confidence in sharing my personal testimony with nonbelievers.

  *Score (1-10):*_____

  My goal for the new year: _____

  _____

- Regularly presenting the gospel message to nonbelievers.

  *Score (1-10):*_____

  On a separate page, list specific people you shared the gospel with this year.

  My goal for the new year: _____

  _____

DISCIPLESHIP

1. Who is investing in me?

2. Whom am I investing in?

3. What are my discipleship goals for the new year?

1. What are my spiritual gifts?

2. On a scale of 1 to 10, how confident do I feel that I am effectively using my spiritual gifts and am trained and equipped to help others discover, develop, and use their spiritual gifts?

    *Score (1-10):*_____

    My goal for the new year: _____

    _____

When Is Your Task Complete?

"When do I know I am finished discipling someone?"

There is no easy answer. Any investment you make in a person's life is valuable. If you can work with a person only for a few months, then do it. If only for a year or so, then by all means, make the commitment. Remember, God is responsible for a person's spiritual growth—not you. You're only a tool in God's hands.

That said, consider the analogy of a parent and a child.

When the child is young, the parent must feed and care for the child and train that child in the fundamentals of daily living, right and wrong, and issues of fundamental character.

As the child grows, a parent becomes more of a coach. The child is in the game of life, and the coach is calling in plays from the sideline, beckoning the child over to offer encouragement and to correct mistakes.

As the child matures into an adult, the parent becomes

less of a coach and more of a partner. Both are now in the game of life together, increasingly as equals and colleagues.

Then one day your child is married and having children and beginning the process all over again.

The same is true with discipleship.

- A discipler might begin as a caregiver for a spiritual infant.
- A discipler becomes a coach for a spiritual adolescent.
- A discipler winds up a colleague of a spiritual adult who becomes a spiritual parent, engaged in spiritual reproduction.

The Cost of *Not* Making Disciples

Many Christians seem to believe that "busyness is next to godliness."

They behave as if moving fast, thinking big, and focusing on the many is a more valuable approach to life than slowing down, thinking small, and faithfully investing in a few. As a result, many Christians—including church leaders—are living lives of speed, exhaustion, and emptiness, not lives of quietness, contentment, and joy.

Moreover, because the faith of many "believers" is no more than skin deep—because they do not have a deep and total commitment to God's Word—the average twenty-first-century church is not having the type of revolutionary social impact that the first-century church had. Tragically, we often see sexual promiscuity, adultery, homosexuality, abortion, divorce, drug and alcohol addiction, dysfunctionality, and depression plaguing our churches just as they are plaguing society at large. The apostle Paul warned us in 2 Timothy 3:5 (NIV) of those "having a form of godliness but denying its power." Yet, sadly, we see evidence of this within the church the world over.

This is the cost of *not* making disciples.

It is certainly true that we have a big world to reach for Christ and that it takes big acts of God to reach it. It's also true that sometimes Jesus and Paul moved fast, thought big, and focused on the many. They wanted to tell the whole world the good news that the Kingdom of God was at hand, accessible to anyone who would truly repent—turn back to God—and trust in the death and resurrection of Jesus Christ for life eternal and abundant. Indeed, we should be no less passionate about reaching our big world than they were.

But preaching to the masses and doing dramatic public miracles were not all that Jesus and Paul did. They made it their mission to make disciples, and thus they dramatically multiplied the impact of their ministries. They built fully devoted, trained, and experienced followers. They invested heavily in these small, select bands of leaders until they were equipped with so much love and so much spiritual capital that they were ready to advance God's Kingdom and radically change the culture, despite intense opposition.

Jesus and Paul were great preachers of the gospel. But neither believed that heralding the Good News was enough. Nor did they believe that helping people enter the Kingdom of God, or even become part of a local church congregation, was enough, not in and of itself.

No, their passion was to reproduce themselves and raise

up more laborers to go into the fields, so white for harvest. Jesus and Paul were looking for far more than devotees; they were looking for dedicated and disciplined disciples—men and women ready, willing, and able to be used by God to lead a global spiritual revolution.

They also understood that such disciples are made, not born.

Faithful followers who can become leaders, guiding others to a deeper, more powerful relationship with the Father, do not grow on trees. They must be recruited and cared for and trained and fashioned and tested by fire.

Jesus' preaching to the masses didn't set the world on fire, though he was the very Word become flesh. What set the world on fire—what ignited the great spiritual revolution known as Christianity—was the handful of disciples that Jesus made and unleashed to go preach the gospel *and* make even more disciples.

There are many ministries to which a person may be called within the context of a healthy, fruitful local church, an "investor" church. But each ministry—whatever it is and wherever it is performed—must have a central mission: making disciples. This is true whether you are a pastor, a missionary, a youth leader, a Sunday school teacher, a music leader, a small-group Bible study leader, or simply a mom, dad, or older brother or sister in Christ.

It is not enough merely to serve in whatever specific ministry area to which God has called you. As God invests in you, you must invest in others. You must know them more deeply, love them more sacrificially, pray with them more regularly, train them more fully, and deploy them more effectively to obey the Great Commandments and fulfill the Great Commission.

This is the invested life.

This is the life to which God has called you.

This is the life that pleases him.

And should you live this life, you will hear him say to you—on that glorious day when you see him face-to-face—the most important twenty-nine words in all of human history:

> Well done, good and faithful servant. You have been faithful with a few things; I will put you in charge of many things. Come and share your master's happiness!
>
> JESUS CHRIST (MATTHEW 25:21, NIV)

Additional Recommended Reading

Here are a few other books on discipleship, leadership, and revival that you may find helpful:

Bakht Singh of India: The Incredible Account of a Modern-Day Apostle by Dr. T. E. Koshy

Implosion: Can America Recover from Its Economic and Spiritual Challenges in Time? by Joel C. Rosenberg

The Training of the Twelve: Timeless Principles for Leadership Development by Alexander B. Bruce

Dedication and Leadership by Douglas Hyde

As Iron Sharpens Iron by Howard Hendricks and William Hendricks

The Cost of Discipleship by Dietrich Bonhoeffer

Twelve Ordinary Men: How the Master Shaped His Disciples for Greatness, and What He Wants to Do with You by John MacArthur

Harvest by Chuck Smith and Tal Brooke

Paul: A Man of Grace and Grit by Charles Swindoll

The Master Disciple-Maker by Hanna Shahin

Discipleship Essentials: A Guide to Building Your Life in Christ by Greg Ogden

About the Authors

JOEL C. ROSENBERG is the *New York Times* bestselling author of seven novels—*The Last Jihad*, *The Last Days*, *The Ezekiel Option*, *The Copper Scroll*, *Dead Heat*, *The Twelfth Imam*, and *The Tehran Initiative*—and three nonfiction books—*Epicenter*, *Inside the Revolution*, and *Implosion*. His books have sold more than 2.5 million copies worldwide. *The Ezekiel Option* received the Gold Medallion Award as the Best Novel of 2006 from the Evangelical Christian Publishers Association. Joel is the producer of two documentary films based on his nonfiction books. He is also the founder of The Joshua Fund, a nonprofit educational and charitable organization to mobilize Christians to "bless Israel and her neighbors in the name of Jesus" with food, clothing, medical supplies, and other humanitarian relief.

As a communications advisor, Joel has worked with a number of U.S. and Israeli leaders, including Steve Forbes, Natan Sharansky, and Benjamin Netanyahu. As an author, he has been interviewed on hundreds of radio and TV programs, including ABC's *Nightline*, CNN, *CNN Headline News*, FOX

News Channel, The History Channel, and MSNBC. He has been profiled by the *New York Times*, the *Washington Times*, the *Jerusalem Post*, and *World* magazine. He has addressed audiences all over the world, including those in Israel, Iraq, Jordan, Egypt, Turkey, Russia, France, Germany, Belgium, and the Philippines. He has also spoken at the White House, the Pentagon, and to members of Congress.

In 2008, Joel designed and hosted the first Epicenter Conference in Jerusalem. The event drew two thousand Christians who wanted to "learn, pray, give, and go" to the Lord's work in Israel and the Middle East. Subsequent Epicenter Conferences have been held in San Diego (2009); Manila, Philippines (2010); Philadelphia (2010); and Jerusalem (2011). His live webcasts of the conferences have drawn more than fifty thousand people from more than one hundred countries.

The son of a Jewish father and a Gentile mother, Joel is an evangelical Christian with a passion to make disciples of all nations and teach Bible prophecy. A graduate of Syracuse University with a BFA in filmmaking, he is married, has four sons, and lives near Washington, D.C.

To visit Joel's weblog—or sign up for his free weekly "Flash Traffic" e-mails—please visit www.joelrosenberg.com.

Please also visit these other websites:

www.joshuafund.net
www.epicenterconference.com

and Joel's "Epicenter Team" and the Joel C. Rosenberg public profile page on Facebook.

DR. T. E. KOSHY is the founder and director of International Friendship Evangelism, has served as the chaplain of evangelical Christian ministries at Syracuse University since 1973, and is the senior pastor of International Assembly, a nondenominational church in Syracuse, New York. He is also one of three senior elders overseeing a movement of some six thousand New Testament–model churches in India, Pakistan, Europe, and Asia.

Brother Bakht Singh of India—Koshy's biography of "the Billy Graham of India"—was originally published in 2003 in India by Operation Mobilization. A paperback edition was published in the United States by InterVarsity Press in 2008.

An internationally recognized leader in cross-cultural evangelism and discipleship training, Dr. Koshy has taught in more than fifty countries. In 1974, he was a participant in the World Evangelism Congress at Lausanne. In 1988, he served as the general secretary of the Billy Graham crusade in Syracuse. In 2000, he preached to an audience of more than 250,000 in his home country of India at the memorial service for Bakht Singh.

Dr. Koshy holds a BA in literature and philosophy and a law degree from the University of Bombay, a degree in theology from Moorland Bible College in London, and an MA in journalism and a PhD in mass communications from Syracuse University.

He and his wife, Indira, live in Syracuse, New York. They have one son, Jay, who is also a pastor making disciples of all nations with his wife and son.

For more information, please go to the following websites:

www.friendshipevangelism.org
www.brotherbakhtsingh.org

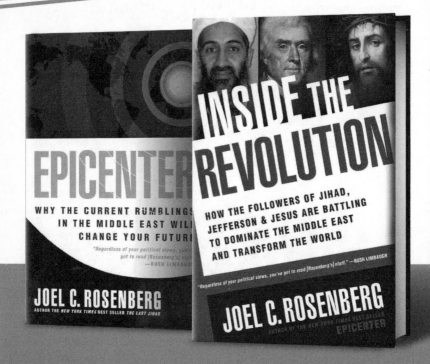

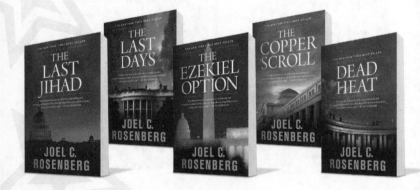